„We see God"

European University Studies
Europäische Hochschulschriften
Publications Universitaires Européennes

**Series XX
Philosophy**

Reihe XX   Série XX
Philosophie
Philosophie

Vol./Bd. 528

PETER LANG
Frankfurt am Main · Berlin · Bern · New York · Paris · Wien

Sigmund Bonk

„We see God"

George Berkeley's Philosophical Theology

PETER LANG
Europäischer Verlag der Wissenschaften

Die Deutsche Bibliothek - CIP-Einheitsaufnahme

Bonk, Sigmund:
„We see God" : George Berkeley's philosophical theology /
Sigmund Bonk. - Frankfurt am Main ; Berlin ; Bern ; New York ;
Paris ; Wien : Lang, 1997
  (European university studies : Ser. 20, Philosophy ; Vol. 528)
  ISBN 3-631-31409-4

NE: Europäische Hochschulschriften / 20

ISSN 0721-3417
ISBN 3-631-31409-4
US-ISBN 0-8204-63252-0

© Peter Lang GmbH
Europäischer Verlag der Wissenschaften
Frankfurt am Main 1997
All rights reserved.

All parts of this publication are protected by copyright. Any
utilisation outside the strict limits of the copyright law, without
the permission of the publisher, is forbidden and liable to
prosecution. This applies in particular to reproductions,
translations, microfilming, and storage and processing in
electronic retrieval systems.

Printed in Germany 1 2   4 5 6 7

Dedicated to my dear mother
Ingeborg Bonk

Acknowledgements

This book was begun in 1993 and completed in 1996. An earlier version of chapter 1 was published as "George Berkeley's Gottesbeweis" in *Neue Zeitschrift für Systematische Theologie und Religionsphilosophie* 36 (1994) pp. 268-283. Chapters 2, 4 and 5 are more or less descended from my hitherto unpublished "Habilitationsschrift" ("Die Verdinglichung der Natur: Berkeley, Hume und der Wandel des Naturbegriffes vor der Industriellen Revolution").

All parts were originally written in German. A translation seemed reasonable to me, as there are probably not so many german-speaking scholars and students interested in Bishop Berkeley's philosophy and theology. Furthermore, there was not even an English monograph on Berkeley's Philosophical Theology - at least to my knowledge.

With regard to the translation I am particularly grateful to my dear relative Mrs. Wendy Bonk, M.A.: thank you! But I am also grateful to Miss Christina Eibl, who translated the "Introduction", the "Conclusion", and some parts of chapter 5. Apart from that, let me here thank Mr. Elmar Singer, M.A., Mr. Georg de Nicolo, M.A., Dipl. oec. Mr. Gottfried Kreckl, Ph. D. Mrs. Elisabeth Angenvoort-Reiß, Mr. Günter Fröhlich, M.A. and Mrs. Brigitta Bitter, too - they know why! But if there should be some bad English left, without doubt I am to blame for this. The reason is that I could not help "improving" the translation at some places...

Waging am See,
August 1996
Sigmund Bonk

Contents

Introduction 11

I. The Argument for the Existence of God (*Principles*) 17
    I.0.   Preliminary remarks 17
    I.1.   Everything we perceive is an idea of sense 18
    I.2.   Ideas of sense cannot be caused by material things 23
    I.3.   We cannot accept that the ideas of sense are produced exclusively in our "limited minds" and only exist there 28
    I.4.   Conclusion: There must be an intellectual being who is superior to us, who creates the ideas of sense, and in whom these ideas exist permanently: God 31

II. The Theory of Objects (*Dialogues*) 33
    II.0.   Preliminary remarks 33
    II.1.   The secondary qualities of a body exist only in the mind 34
    II.2.   The primary qualities of a body are essentially the same as the secondary qualities. 39
    II.3.   A body does not consist of any additional "material substance" other than its perceptible qualities 43
    II.4.   A body is nothing but an isolated bundle of perceptible qualities - created to make life possible 48

III. The Argument for a Divine Providence (*New Theory*) 51
    III.0.   Preliminary remarks 51
    III.1.   Berkeley's thesis that visual ideas of sense are a language of God and a primary means of his providence 53
    III.2.   George Berkeley's main argument for his thesis of the total disparity between the objects of the visual and the tactile senses . 57

III.3. A short discussion of Berkeley's main argument and our suggestion for a solution of the problem of visual depth perception ... 59

 III.4. Concluding notes ... 62

IV. The Argument for God's Activity in Nature (*De motu*) ... 65

 IV.0. Preliminary remarks ... 65

 IV.1. Berkeley's "instrumentalist" tendencies in his philosophy of language ... 66

 IV.2. Force (Power) and motion in *De motu* ... 69

 IV.3. Berkeley as a precursor of Duhem ... 73

 IV.4. The idea of a visible God ... 78

V. The Theory of Time and Mind (*Philosophical Commentaries*) ... 83

 V.0. Preliminary remarks ... 83

 V.1. The theory of time in the *Philosophical Commentaries* ... 84

 V.2. Time and divinity ... 87

 V.3. Berkeley's conception of the mind and the "Lockean objection" ... 91

 V.4. Time, self and freedom ... 96

Conclusion ... 103

Zusammenfassung in deutscher Sprache ... 105

Literature ... 107

Introduction

The following interpretation of the main philosophical works of the Irish Bishop George Berkeley (1685-1753) intends to take serious the religious aspect of his works which has quite often been neglected. There can be no such thing as **the** valid interpretation of an artistic or philosophical work - we do not mean to question that hermeneutic maxim. This does not exclude, however, that some interpretations get closer to their author's own intentions than others. They are not for this only reason "better" (and more interesting), but contribute more to the understanding of a historical figure. Often this figure can hardly demand any interest of his own, fading completely in importance behind the work (one might probably think of Immanuel Kant here). When this is the case, the interest in an interpretation focusing on original intention decreases accordingly.

Berkeley **was** a person of public life, particularly after he had been appointed Lord Bishop in 1734. But even before that time he had repeatedly "interfered" in social and political life: by means of his fellowship in Dublin and his sermons, by accompanying Lord Peterborough, the ambassador extraordinary, to Italy (1713/1714), as the Dean of Derry (since 1724), as a member of the House of Lords, as a political author supporting the Tories, as the initiator of the "Bermuda Project", i.e. the (failed) plan for the foundation of a college for future missionaries in the Bermudas (leading Berkeley to Rhode Island in 1728) which repeatedly preoccupied the government and Parliament, by being a co-founder of the later "Columbia University", with his pro-American poem "Westwards" (which earned him "patronage" of Berkeley University in California), with his much-observed criticism of intellectuals and "freethinkers" in *Alciphron* (1732), through his close friendship with Jonathan Swift and his literary and political circle (since his student days in Dublin already), with his national-economic writings (*The Querist* in particular, between 1735 and 1737) which were above all intended for the improvement of Ireland's economic situation, by inventing and propagating "tar water", an alleged miracle cure that initiated the fashion of tar water drinking in about half of all European countries (since the publication of *Siris* in 1744), with his writings that are important from a scientific and historical point of view that goes beyond the mere history of medicine: *The New Theory of Vision* (1709*)*, *De motu* (1721), and *The Analyst* (1734), not to forget his well-known opposition to Newton and the contemporary uncritical enthusiasm for

Newton's person.[1] Berkeley's latter scientific contribution to the culture of his time already touches on our issue "Berkeley as a Philosopher", from which the treatment of the scattered philosophical remarks in the *Querist*, the *Analyst*, and *Siris* shall be excluded though.

Thus, our topic and the nature of our task have been framed quite accurately already: Berkeley's main philosophical works (with the exception of *Alciphron*- more a summary than a new separate work), the *Philosophical Commentaries*, *A New Theory of Vision*, *The Principles of Human Knowledge*, the *Three Dialogues Between Hylas and Philonous* and *De motu* shall be interpreted in five chapters that are meant to mutually complement and illuminate each other. This will be done in perspective of Berkeley's strong personal belief in God. For, he was not primarily concerned with the themes and phenomena his name has again and again been associated with by various historians of philosophy, as for example "empiricism", "phenomenalism", "idealism", "nominalism", "positivism", "analysis" etc.; he was rather concerned with guiding his readers to **God** and **duty**. This is also what he himself asserts, and not only at some random place but in the final paragraph of his main philosophical work, the *Principles*. It runs as follows:

> For after all, what deserves the first place in our studies, is the consideration of *God*, and our *duty*; which to promote, as it was the main drift and design of my labours, so shall I esteem them altogether useless and ineffectual, if by what I have said I cannot inspire my readers with a pious sense of the presence of God: and having shewn the falseness or vanity of those barren speculations, which make the chief employment of learned men, the better dispose them to reverence and embrace the salutary truths of the Gospel, which to know and to practice is the highest perfection of human nature.[2]

Readers should be "inspired with an increased pious sense of the presence of God" - this was what mattered above all to Bishop Berkeley. And thus he wanted to prove that God is indeed always present (and that we, bearing in mind

---

[1] More biographical information can be found in A.A. Luce, *The Life of George Berkeley, Bishop of Cloyne*, London 1949.

[2] Ayers (Ed.), p. 127, (*Principles* § 156). The quotations from Berkeley's works are taken from the widely used and highly reliable "Everyman Library" edition: *Berkeley, Philosophical Works Including the Works on Vision*, ed. Michael R. Ayers, London 1985. Paragraphs, numbers, sections and parts of the original structure will also be given so that other editions can be used for comparison. (Ayer's text follows the standard edition by A.A. Luce and T.E. Jessop: George Berkeley, Bishop of Cloyne, Works in 9 Volumes, London and Edinburgh 1948-51.)

that presence, should refrain from violating his commandments, i.e. from acting against our "duty"). It is astonishing how few interpreters have recognized this thought that seems to suggest itself as Berkeley's crucial one, and also the fundamental intention connected with it. But probably they recognized it and only considered the obvious thing as too little original and not "worthy" enough of being depicted? We do not know it, and do not want to care too much about the correct answer. Instead, we are glad of having discovered one interpreter at least who clearly expresses the obvious thing.

In his essay "L'intuition philosophique" *Henri Bergson* claims that all important philosophies are based on a particular fundamental intuition which is always very simple (though not easily expressed), and already contains the whole system in a nutshell:

> Dans le cas de Berkeley, je crois voir deux images différentes, et celle qui me frappe le plus n'est pas celle dont nous trouvons l'indication complète chez Berkeley lui-même. Il me semble que Berkeley aperçoit la matière comme une *mince pellicule transparente* située entre l'homme et Dieu. Elle reste transparent tant que les philosophes ne s'occupent pas d'elle, et alors Dieu se montre au travers. Mais que les métaphysiciens y touchent, ou même le sens commun en tant qu'il est métaphysicien: aussitôt la pellicule se dépolit et s'épaissit, devient opaque et forme écran, parce que des mots tels que Substance, Force, Etendue abstraite, etc., se glissent derrière elle, s'y déposent comme une couche de poussière, et nous empêchent d'apercevoir Dieu par transparence. L'image est à peine indiquée par Berkeley lui-même, quoiqu'il ait dit en propres termes «que nous soulevons la poussière et que nous nous plaignons ensuite de ne pas voir». Mais il y a une autre comparaison, souvent évoquée par le philosophe, et qui n'est que la transposition auditive de l'image visuelle que je viens de décrire: la matière serait une langue que Dieu nous parle. Les métaphysiques de la matière, épaississant chacune des syllabes, lui faisant un sort, l'érigeant en entité indépendante, détourneraient alors notre attention du sens sur le son et nous empêcheraient de suivre la parole divine. Mais, qu'on s'attache à l'une ou à l'autre, dans les deux cas on a affaire à une image simple qu'il faut garder sous les yeux, parce que, si elle n'est pas l'intuition génératrice de la doctrine, elle en dérive immédiatement et s'en rapproche plus qu'aucune des thèses prise à part, plus même que leur combinaison. [3]

---

[3] Henri Bergson, "L'intuition philosophique", in: Henri Gouhier (Ed.), *H. Bergson-Oeuvres*, Paris 1963, pp. 13-56.

According to that Berkeley did not simply "deny" matter (corporality) as can usually be read (what would be gained by such a crazy idea?), but he interpreted it newly, namely as a (primarily visual) language by which God speaks to us and, possibly more clearly, as a kind of thin, transparent skin that is spread out between two different spiritual beings, namely God and the (each) human individual. Considered in more detail, the idea is that we can see God through this delicate, diaphanous medium if we look at physical nature in the right (contemplative) manner. In a similar way we believe to be perceiving something "noumenous" (R. Otto) and divine when admiring the works of great landscape or still life painters.[4] Or, in a similar manner we believe to recognize something of a person's mind and soul when looking at his or her face and eyes ... Just as the human spirit can become visible in a face, the divine spirit can in nature. We could this divine becoming perceptible in our physical world or nature call the "visible God". (Berkeley himself bluntly says in the *Principles*, Sect. 148: "**we see god**".)

Just as Bergson, Arthur Schopenhauer (and before him F. W. J. Schelling) and many mystics knew about intuitive contemplation of the supernatural in nature which he (Schopenhauer but not quite unlike Berkeley) calls "idea". **Idea** is contrasted with **concept**, the former being vivid, the latter definite. The ideas' contemplation is disturbed by the thinking in concepts; the idea becomes visible only when one does no longer observe natural objects in a rational way, but completely devotes oneself to their "immediate" contemplation.

> Wenn man, durch die Kraft des Geistes gehoben, die gewöhnliche Betrachtungsart der Dinge fahren läßt, aufhört, nur ihren Relationen zu einander, deren letztes Ziel immer die Relation zum eigenen Willen ist, am Leitfaden der Gestaltungen des Satzes vom Grunde, nachzugehn, also nicht mehr das Wo, das Wann, das Warum und das Wozu an den Dingen betrachtet; sondern einzig und allein das W a s ; auch nicht das abstrakte Denken, die Begriffe der Vernunft, das Bewußtseyn einnehmen läßt; sondern, statt alles diesen, die ganze Macht seines Geistes der Anschauung hingiebt, sich ganz in diese versenkt und das ganze Bewußtsein ausfüllen läßt durch die ruhige Kontemplation des gerade gegenwärtigen natürlichen Gegenstandes, sei es eine Landschaft, ein Baum, ein Fels, ein Gebäude oder was auch immer; indem man, nach einer sinnvollen Deutschen Redensart, sich gänzlich in diesen Gegenstand verliert, d.h. eben sein Individuum, seinen Willen, vergißt und nur noch als reines Subjekt, als wahrer Spiegel des

---

[4] Berkeley was himself a lover of painting and even owned works of Rubens and Van Dyck.

> Objekts bestehen bleibt; so, daß es ist, als ob der Gegenstand allein dawäre, ohne Jemanden, der ihn wahrnimmt, und man also nicht mehr den Anschauenden von der Anschauung trennen kann, sondern Beide Eines geworden sind, indem das ganze Bewußtseyn von einem einzigen anschaulichen Bilde gänzlich gefüllt und eingenommen ist; wenn also solchermaßen das Objekt aus aller Relation zu etwas außer ihm, das Subjekt aus aller Relation zum Willen getreten ist: dann ist, was also erkannt wird, nicht mehr das einzelne Ding als solches; sondern es ist die I d e e, [...] [5]

Certainly, these thoughts go beyond Berkeley's explicit explanations (cf. however the "First Draft" to his Introduction to the *Principles*). We do not yet assert that Schopenhauer and Berkeley say exactly the same thing. What we do maintain though is the following: that the Irish Bishop - regardless of his great mathematical talent, his clear-cut arguments and usually somewhat prosaic style - belongs under this surface mainly to the intuitionist-mystic, and not to the rationalist-positivist tradition of philosophy. According to their real intention and their basic intuition Berkeley's works can be classed as belonging in a line with the "neoplatonists, Bonaventura, Böhme, Cudworth, Schelling, Schopenhauer, Lotze, Bergson, Husserl, and the phenomenologists" rather than, as it has usually been done so far, with the "atomists, Bacon, Locke, Hume, Mill, Mach, Russell, and the analytic philosophers".

---

[5] Arthur Schopenhauer, Zurich edition, Vol. 1, p. 231 (*Die Welt als Wille und Vorstellung* I, "Drittes Buch", § 34).

I. The Argument for the Existence of God (*Principles*)

I.0. Preliminary remarks

In 1710 the 25 year old Irish philosopher George Berkeley, who was later to become an Anglican bishop, published his major work *A Treatise Concerning the Principles of Human Knowledge*.[6] Up to the present this has almost always been studied from an epistemological point of view.[7] As a contribution to the theory of knowledge it is of such brilliant clarity from an argumentative point of view, that the metaphysical (or even mystical) aspect in a broader sense can easily be overlooked. In actual fact this book can also be regarded as a contribution to rational or philosophical theology, captivating the reader through its original boldness. At the same time these two aspects are not mutually exclusive. On the contrary, more intensive studies of *The Principles of Human Knowledge* reveal that the argumentation for immaterialism - an epistemological (and ontological) position beyond objectivist realism **and** subjectivist idealism as will be shown - is at the same time an argumentation for the existence of God. The final paragraph 156 characterizes - not without good reason - Berkeley's aim as being a moral and religious one. (Once more:)

> For after all, what deserves the first place in our studies, is the consideration of *God*, and our *duty*; which to promote, as it was the main drift and design of my labours, so shall I esteem them altogether useless and ineffectual, if by what I have said I cannot inspire my readers with a pious sense of the presence of God [...] [8]

The arguments in the *Principles*, considered as contributions to rational theology, are hardly systematic despite the fact that all paragraphs are individually lucid and that some are explicitly pointing to religious subjects. We think nevertheless that a relatively simple proof structure can be found which underlies the whole argumentation that has become entangled by the prima facie more or less continuous change of thoughts. The aim of this proof lies in the statement that there is a divine spirit who created our world (which is a world made up of "ideas" as "real atoms") out of his own ideas and continuously maintains its (their) existence.

---

[6] In: Ayers (Ed.), pp. 61-127
[7] Two exceptions are: Jonathan Bennett, *Locke, Berkeley, Hume: Central Themes*, Oxford 1971, Ch. 7 and John L. Mackie, *The Miracle of Theism*, Oxford 1982, Ch. 4.
[8] Cf. our footnote 2.

1. Premise: Everything that we perceive is an idea of sense.
2. Premise: Ideas of sense cannot be caused by material objects
3. Premise: We cannot assume that ideas of sense are created solely by our limited minds and only exist there.
Conclusion: There must be an intellectual being, far superior to us who creates the ideas of sense and in whom these ideas exist permanently: (The appropriate expression for such a mind is the word) "God".

Obviously, all the premises leading to this conclusion need essentially to be explained and (as far as possible) justified. The major part of this first chapter deals with this task.

I.1. Everything we perceive is an idea of sense

Berkeley adopts the notion "idea" from John Locke who differentiates between atoms as elements of nature and ideas as elements of mind. The ideas of sense, unlike the ideas of reflection, exist in the mind through mediation of the external senses. According to Locke, these ideas of sense are pictures or representations of objects, or more precisely, of qualities of material (atomic) substances. The awkward consequence of this so-called representational theory of perception is well-known: we can never be sure that our mental pictures (or ideas of sense respectively) are really identical with the objects in the external world. For, as we have no access whatsoever to the external world which has not been conveyed to us by ideas, we do not have any possibility of comparing our ideas with objects in the external world and with their attributes. Berkeley already tries to avoid this problem in the first paragraphs of *The Principles of Human Knowledge*. Both philosophers have the same starting point: regardless of what we perceive, these perceptions are not transcending the mind but always are "immanent". However, Berkeley is already stepping straight onto unexplored philosophical terrain in these first paragraphs. He makes claims here that have never been made before and even today such claims sound still "outrageous": these ideas of sense, being the immediate objects of perception, are the elements of sensual consciousness **and at the same time nature's building stones ("real atoms")**!

> And as several of these are observed to accompany each other, they come to be marked by one name, and so to be reputed as one thing. Thus, for example, a certain colour, taste, smell, figure and consistence

[all ideas of sense, S. B.] having been observed to go together, are accounted one distinct thing, signified by the name *apple*.[9]

If objects themselves consist of "ideas of sense", then the problem of how we can know that our ideas of sense are similar to the objects in themselves does not arise. Obviously, there is at once a possible objection to Berkeley's point of view: there are significant differences between ideas and objects, which "fact" lets such a determined identification appear absurd from the beginning. Ideas of sense are only identical with sensible "objects" in hallucinations and similar occurrences. A hallucinated loaf of bread and a real one are for instance clearly distinguishable by the fact that the latter will nourish a starving person and keep him alive.

We think that this objection should be taken for serious. However, Berkeley possibly can be defended, if we consider him as having replaced the concept of the identity of ideas of sense and sensible objects by one of **partial identity**. My ideas of sense are only **completely identical** with their objects if they occur in my hallucinations or my dreams. This does not imply though that my ideas have always to be as it were image representations - they could indeed be part of the object itself. After I have helped myself to a piece of cake I do not have a representation of the cake on my plate, but merely some part of it. This might also be true in the case of perception: an object is identical with a bundle of (God's) ideas and this in turn - if we are to understand Berkeley[10] - is identical with the sum of all possible images that we could possibly have of the object. If I have an object in front of me, e.g. an apple, I can get several different perceptions of it but I would never have all the possible perceptions at once at the same time. Therefore, an identity between the "real" object of my sensation and the object which I presently perceive immediately (i.e. the idea or ideas of sense), never exists on the one hand (I do not have a precise idea of the inside of the apple for instance). And yet on the other hand, there is never a representational relationship either. What does exist though is a relationship of **partial** identity.

---

[9] Ayers (Ed.), p. 77 (*Priniples*, § 1).
[10] As Berkeley clearly knew about the "unpleasant (sceptical) consequences" of the representational theory of perception mentioned above, we have to assume that he took the difference between God's ideas of sense and those of his created beings as merely quantitative and not qualitative. Even where the quality of these ideas is concerned, there should be no unsurpassable difference between their potential realization in the mind of God and in the mind of created humans (if the following unpleasant sceptical consequence of the true nature of things in the unrecognizable outside world is to be avoided: we know nothing about these things in themselves {the things outside the realm of our consciousness} - not even whether they have existence ...).

Berkeley's thesis about natural objects, that are composed of ideas of sense, can also be rephrased, stating that the philosopher denies the existence of "material substances". These were, according to Locke, the constituents or supporters (substrata) of the different qualities which were to be found in the manner or modus of ideas in the mind. When we first catch sight of an apple for instance, and pick it up then, we would usually be convinced - should we be asked to give information about it - that the objects (correlata obiectiva) of our visual and tactile perceptions have the same material composition, that is, the atomic or material substance of the apple. According to Berkeley such material quality "supporters" do not exist: the reason why we always experience some perceptions in association with each other lies simply in the fact that they are connected in the first place in God's own mind: and if God "perceives" (per analogiam) every event in some way or other, then everything is "in him", carried by his spirit - and this means that Locke's hypothesis simply would be **redundant**.

However, we should not anticipate the results of Berkeley's argumentation too often. Let us rather take a further look at Berkeley's ideas about the relations between the individual senses, the ideas of sense and their specific objects or "immediate" objects. Let us imagine that we are in a room where the windows face onto a dark street. It seems to us that we can hear a horse trotting along that street. Now it is certainly conceivable (though probably highly improbable) that someone runs down the street quickly and imitates the sound of a trotting horse cleverly in some way. That means that we could not say, for instance in a law court where a precise statement is required, that we had heard a horse trotting. Strictly speaking, we could only claim to have heard the noise of a trotting horse and to have thought of a horse as the material object connected with this sound. Berkeley describes this situation in his first publication *A New Theory of Vision* in the following way: the actual, "proper object" of our sense of hearing is made up of sounds and tones. The analogy is valid for the following (more up-to-date) situation: I can for instance smell a lavender bush in the darkness. And yet I can not exclude the possibility that it might only be some synthetically-produced fragrance spray from a can. Again, I have to state that I smell the **scent** or **smell of lavender**, but not a material object such as the **lavender bush**. Correspondingly, the "proper object" of the sense of taste is the actual taste. Therefore, Berkeley says that every sense has its own correlative and specific sensation.

But it has probably been noticed already that the association of sense and the object of sense in the concept pairs "sense of hearing - sound", "sense of smell - smell" and "sense of taste - taste" seems quite natural as the appropriate expressions come to the mind of an English speaker quite easily. Finding appropriate expressions to complete the analogies with the visual and tactile senses is certainly far more difficult. Somehow we object to supporting Berkeley in his claim that we really only feel differing resistance (which in turn gives us impressions of hardness, softness etc.) and that we only see impressions of light and colour. G. J. Warnock writes in this context: "I heard the sound of a car; I smelled the smell of the geraniums; I saw the ... of a tree. There is no expression that fills the gap in the last of these sentences, in the way in which "sound" and "smell" find an ordinary natural place in the others".[11] (Warnock could have replaced the sentence *I saw the ... of a tree* with the sentence *I felt the ... of a tree*). It would be - to say the very least - stilted and bad English to say "I saw the light and colour impression of a tree". Our habit of associating visual ideas of existing objects with the objects themselves is accepted and "founded" in the very grammar of our language. This is also true for the objects of our tactile sense. To begin with, Berkeley thinks that it is intuitively unintelligible that the visual and tactile senses should not also have their "specific" or proper objects. Why should only these different senses share the same ("material") object?

The rather complicated argumentative string of Berkeley's thesis to the effect that such a common object does not exist, can be found above all in his first philosophical work, the *New Theory of Vision*.[12] It cannot be repeated here in any great detail. We will limit ourselves therefore to discussing at least two of the reasons which are - according to Berkeley - responsible for the misguided opinion that there has to be a material constituent as an object identical with our visual and tactile perceptions. The first reason is our belief: where we can clearly see an apple, there has necessarily to be an apple that we can touch and vice versa. Berkeley points out that there is an often neglected, but important difference between necessity as it is found in logical and mathematical conclusions, and the mere feeling of necessity as it occurs when certain associations are repeatedly experienced.[13] Berkeley speaks of necessary connections such as those found in mathematics, in logic and sometimes in philosophy (which can be classified under the modern concept of an "analytical necessity") when referring to associations which are inseparable even in the imagination (in the sense of "the mind"). For example: I cannot **imagine** (in a broad sense, mental pictures are not necessarily included here) a whole number which is neither divisible by 2 nor becomes divisible by 2 through the addition of 1. It is also impossible for me to imagine an

---

[11] G.J. Warnock, *Berkeley*, Oxford 1983³, p. 37.
[12] *An Essay Towards a New Theory of Vision*, Dublin 1709¹. In: Ayers (Ed.), pp. 1-59. (Cf. also our Chapter II).
[13] A good account of this idea with text references in: Arend Kulenkampff, *George Berkeley*, Munich 1987¹, pp. 62-64.

angle that can be closed to a triangle by two (different) straight lines. Neither can I conceive of a colour which is not extended. This analytical necessity is the only necessity in the strict sense of the word. However, sometimes the expression "natural necessity" can be heard. This must be understood as to cover associations of events such as the dropping of an apple and its falling, or the throwing of a piece of paper into the fire and its burning up. All these associations are, however, easily separated in the mind and do not have to be true for all possible worlds. Just think of the two events of catching sight of an apple and feeling a relatively smooth surface and a relatively large resistance at the point where the visual impression of the apple is localised. The assumption that material substances of objects certainly exist has a lot to do with the intuitive feeling of that only so-called "necessity" (necessary connection) of such associations or ideas. If we are aware that we can distinguish between two types of necessity, by which, strictly speaking, the mere **feeling** of the necessity of connected events does not represent any necessarily connected events at all, then we would possibly be more prepared for taking greater notice of interpretations of the external world such as Berkeley's.[14]

A second reason (linked to the first one) for the opinion that visual and tactile-haptic perceptions are based on one and the same "material substratum" lies, according to Berkeley, in an **internalised projection performance** that is carried out by adults virtually automatically. At the very moment that I am confronted with certain visual ideas of sense, I often read certain haptic ideas of sense into them: e.g. I see an unknown object that is white, indistinct, has blurred edges and reminds me of cotton wool. I say "that looks soft". Or I see a chair that glazes and has very distinct contours. I think to myself, "that looks hard". Through these usually unconsciously drawn close associations of visual impressions and haptic "meanings", the idea of a seemingly self-evident fact is nurtured further. That means that an identical something does exist of which the visual and haptic perceptions are only like two perceivable sides of one medal. However, strictly speaking, it is certainly nonsense to impose visual impressions with predicates taken from the haptic area. To put it very clearly: Berkeley's denial of the connection of our ideas with material substances does (or need) not mean that he denies the existence of corporeal objects in "real nature"

---

[14] It is possible to expand Berkeley's argumentation by reminding of the fact that this is even more the case because some things do exist which - although visible - are untouchable, e.g. rainbows and colours in general (*color* not *pigmentum*). Berkeley would say that all that is visible is, strictly speaking, untouchable: We will learn that for him visible and tactile ideas occupy different spaces.

respectively in "God's mind". Even if these objects were said to exist only as "collections of ideas"[15], they still remain as real as ever.

> All things that exist, exist only in the mind, that is, they are purely notional. What therefore becomes of the sun, moon, and stars? What must we think of houses, rivers, mountains, trees, stones; nay even of our own bodies? Are all these but so many chimeras and illusions of the fancy? To all which, and whatever else of the same sort may be objected, I answer, that by the principles premised, we are not deprived of any one thing in Nature. Whatever we see, feel, hear, or any wise conceive or understand, remains as secure as ever, and is as real as ever. There is a *rerum natura* [...] The only thing whose existence we deny, is that which philosophers call matter or corporeal substance.[16]

The sentence "everything we perceive is an idea of sense" has now been explained and thus substantiated. "Substantiated" because we have seen that there is no contradiction between this sentence and the sentence we may at first have considered more plausible - "everything we perceive is an object". The former now proves to be merely the stricter philosophical expression.

I.2. Ideas of sense cannot be caused by material things

In the second premise of Berkeley's proof of the existence of God the ideas of sense (actually and immediately experienced light-colour impressions, sounds, smells etc.) are discussed again. At first it was stated that we always perceive only these consciously immanent ideas of sense, and never material objects or their qualities *per se*. Then Berkeley goes a step further in the direction of his actual aim (the proof of the existence of God): seemingly existent consciousness-transcending things cannot even be regarded as being causally responsible for the ideas of sense.

His first argumentative string begins in paragraph 8 of the *Principles* where Berkeley confronts the advocates of the adverse theory with the following problem:

> Again, I ask whether those supposed originals or external things, of which our ideas are the pictures or representations, be themselves

---
[15] For "collections of ideas", cf. in: Ayers (Ed.), p. 77 (*Priniples*, § 1).
[16] Ayers (Ed.), p. 86 f. (*Priniples*, §§ 34 and 35).

perceivable or no? If they are, then they are ideas, and we have gained our point; but if you say they are not, I appeal to anyone whether it be sense, to assert a colour is like something which is invisible; hard or soft, like something which is intangible; and so of the rest. [17]

After asking such questions, which certainly put the materialists [18] at least into a certain predicament, Berkeley continues with an attack on the division of an object into the two aspects of "material substance" and "qualities". In actual fact such a division seems not only artificial, but also poses us with the problem of having somehow to understand the kind of relationship that exists between the substance (or the substratum) and the qualities (accidentiae).

> But let us examine a little the received opinion. It is said extension is a mode or accident of matter, and that matter is the *substratum* that supports it. Now I desire that you would explain what is meant by matter's *supporting* extension: say you, I have no idea of matter, and therefore cannot explain it. I answer, though you have no positive, yet if you have any meaning at all, you must at least have a relative idea of matter [19]; though you know not what it is, yet you must be supposed to know what relation it bears to accidents, and what is meant by its supporting them. It is evident *support* cannot here be taken in its usual or literal sense, as when we say that pillars support a building: in what sense therefore must it be taken? [20]

The first string of arguments for this thesis about the ideas of sense, which cannot be caused by material things, is brought to a conclusion in Berkeley's criticism of the concept of "mere space". [21] It is supposed to accommodate the alleged causes of ideas of sense, the things in themselves or material substances. Such an absolute space would be "space itself", and that is to say, it would neither be perceivable, nor would there be (so Berkeley maintains - we will return to this question) arguments for postulating its existence. There is a more decisive argument, however: space cannot even be imagined without the idea of objects of sense - which means that the concept of absolute space proves to be (according to

---

[17] Cf. Ayers (Ed.), p. 79.
[18] Throughout this essay the expression "materialism" refers to the ontological thesis that material things (matter) exist (exists), and not to the reductionist thesis that holds that all that exists is material things (matter).
[19] "You must at least have a relative idea of matter" - Cf. the German translation (Meiners Phil. Bibliothek, 33): "so darf doch zum mindesten eine negative [sic!] nicht fehlen" - "one negative at least must not be missing."
[20] Ayers (Ed.), p. 81 (*Principles*, § 16).
[21] Ayers (Ed.), p. 113 (*Priniples*, § 116).

an empiricist theory of meaning) a meaningless concept. Space itself (or real spaces - cf. below) is not an existent container of matter or things existing in themselves; it is only constituted by the relationship between the ideas of sense (of different kinds) which make up corporeal things (and exist in the first place in the divine spirit).

A second string of arguments is related to the concept of causation. Berkeley poses the question of how we really experience effective causality. He suggests that, looking at the matter with close focus, we only experience this in relation to the mind, that is, primarily through introspection. It does actually seem indisputable at first that we continually experience ourselves as the cause of different events.[22] But then, do we not experience inanimate objects as the cause of various objects in the same way? Berkeley's answer is - in his wish to be more exact or to take the matter strictly empirically - "no". "All our ideas, sensations, or the things which we perceive, by whatsoever names they may be distinguished, are visibly inactive".[23] Does this not clearly contradict our everyday experience? Berkeley would say it contradicts only what we assume unthinkingly to be our everyday experience. The things we are actually able to perceive, are regularities in the succession of certain ideas, that is all. "For when we perceive certain ideas of sense constantly followed by other ideas, and we know that this is not of our own doing, we forthwith attribute power and agency to the ideas themselves, and make one the cause of another, than which nothing can be more absurd or unintelligible".[24] We consider ourselves to be the cause of events and then make this twofold mistake: we firstly identify ourselves with our own bodies and, because they are in certain ways similar to other corporeal elements of nature, secondly read into the latter the power of causation. This procedure seems absurd and unjustifiable to Berkeley. Sensual information cannot be caused by material things because on the one hand the concept of the material thing with its particular characteristics and consequences is extremely problematic (these things being unrecognisable in themselves, the mysterious partition of these same things into substratum and accidentiae, the concept of "absolute" space itself), and on the other hand there is, under "strict" (self-)perception, no causal activity of all things that are not minds or spirits.

---

[22] Therefore, looking at the matter this way, it seems not necessary to have a philosophical proof of freedom, but the determinist has to prove his case.
[23] Ayers (Ed.), p. 84 (*Principles*, § 25).
[24] Ayers (Ed.), p. 86 (*Principles*, § 32). Might have Hume learnt his lesson on causation here?

A third argumentative string connects paragraph 19 with paragraph 85. According to paragraph 19 of the *Principles*[25] the thesis that material objects are the cause of our ideas of sense, contributes nothing to our understanding of the formation of such ideas in our mind. According to a suggestion in paragraph 85[26], this very thesis even makes the phenomenon completely inconceivable. In the already mentioned paragraph 19 Berkeley writes:

> [...] for though we give the materialists their external bodies, they by their own confession are never the nearer knowing how our ideas are produced: since they own themselves unable to comprehend in what manner body can act upon spirit, or how it is possible it should imprint any idea in the mind.

It is possible to be of the opinion that this statement of Berkeley's has in principle kept its relevance despite all scientific research that has been carried out so intensively in the meantime. Probably no brain physiologist, empirical psychologist or other scientist would dare to claim today that he knew how the "transfer" of material stimuli to conscious experience takes place. This becomes an even more critical problem when we refer - as Berkeley himself does in this connection - to the fact that it is possible to have conscious experiences without the influence of external material objects as it is the case in dreams and hallucinations. The materialist-minded theorist of perception would then also have to explain how two completely different starting positions (on the one hand with the substantial occurrence of material objects, and on the other without it) can lead to an intrinsically identical awareness of an experienced situation (at least during the dream or hallucination). Obviously, such objections are not intended (certainly not by Berkeley who was in general well-disposed towards rationality and science) to question the value of the empirical study of perception, which has undoubtedly amongst other things produced some impressive results in discovering many of the physical (chemical, bio-physiological) mechanisms involved in conscious experiences. However, there does not seem to exist any physical mechanism which is (or could be) capable of transforming physical, material stimuli into conscious experience. Berkeley's argumentation reaches its first peak in the thought that accepting the existence of material causes for the explanation of our ideas of sense raises an insoluble dilemma. Indeed, what we have here is of course the "mind-body" problem, definitely well-known to all philosophers.[27]

---

[25] Ayers (Ed.), p. 82.
[26] Ayers (Ed.), p. 103.
[27] Cf. Ayers (Ed.), *Principles*, § 85. As I tried to show in more detail in my doctoral thesis *Immaterialismus: Darstellung und Verteidigung von George Berkeleys Gottesbeweis*

At this point Berkeley's most famous argument must finally be mentioned. It is often referred to as his "master argument". According to it[28], there is already a peculiar contradiction in itself in the concept of a consciousness-transcending material substance or a thing considered in itself. Berkeley's strategy in this master argument then generally consists in rendering absurd the concept of a material thing (not necessarily: of a real or corporeal thing in God's spirit). It should be obvious that neither the statement that ideas of sense are caused by material things, nor even the statement that they are somehow connected with material things, make any good sense if the concept of material things turns out to involve a contradiction in itself. According to Berkeley, this is exactly the case: "[...] that upon a narrow inquiry, it will not perhaps be found, so many as is imagined do really believe the existence of matter or things without the mind. Strictly speaking, to believe that which involves a contradiction, or has no meaning in it, is impossible".[29] A similar statement can be traced in the *Philosophical Commentaries*.

> The Philosophers Talk much of a distinction twixt absolute & relative things, or twixt things consider'd in their own nature & the same thing considered with respect to us [to spirits, S.B.]. I know now w^t they mean by things consider'd in themselves. This is nonsense, Jargon.[30]

In paragraph 24[31] Berkeley entreats the reader, whilst trying to understand objects in themselves or external to the (every) mind or spirit, to "calmly attend to their own thoughts". By urging the reader to do this, Berkeley wants to explain why it can be accepted in the beginning that the expression "things in themselves", unlike expressions such as "round rectangle" and "unmarried husband", does not contain a contradiction in the basic word combination. However, there are, besides these semantic contradictions, also pragmatic ones between the content of the thought and the performance. The performance of thoughts such as "I do not exist" or "I do not speak a word of English" gives rise to such contradictions. It is obvious that the point Berkeley is making here, is that

---

und immaterialistischem Weltbild, München 1990, Part II. Chap. 3, one of the most important arguments for Berkeley's theory is that he can dispose of the mind-body problem to a large extent.

[28] Cf. Ayers (Ed.), p. 83 f. (*Principles*, §§ 22-24) and additionally *Three Dialogues between Hylas and Philonous*, First Dialogue. In: Ayers (Ed.), p. 158 (Luce and Jessop, Eds., p. 200).

[29] Ayers (Ed.), p. 93 (*Principles*, § 54).

[30] The *Philosophical Commentaries* are notebooks written in early life. Berkeley himself did not publish or think of publishing them, this might explain the sloppy style. Citation: Ayers (Ed.), p. 331 (*Philosophical Commentaries*, No. 832).

[31] Ayers (Ed.), p. 84.

the performance of the thought "I think of, respectively I imagine an object external to my mind" contains just such a "pragmatic" contradiction (in thinking of it, it is somehow in my mind). However, a thought that contains a contradiction cannot possibly be true. If we can neither imagine an object transcendent to our minds (or the **absolute** existence of an object respectively), nor think of it without contradiction, then the materialists[32] simply lose the basic preconditions necessary for accounting for their position.[33]

I.3. We cannot accept that the ideas of sense are produced exclusively in our "limited minds" and only exist there

Berkeley's "master argument" goes a long way towards substantiating his proof of the existence of God. Everything we (immediately) perceive is (called) an idea of sense and so there can be no doubt that we do indeed perceive these ideas. Berkeley shared the traditional belief that ideas of sense must draw their existence as contingent beings from somewhere else, that is to say, they cannot come into existence spontaneously out of their own making (and they are related to an actively perceiving mind). Neither accepting other ideas of sense - ideas of sense being experienced as completely inactive - as the cause or causes of these ideas, nor referring to material substances, gives us a satisfactory explanation: the latter in particular so because, according to the master argument, the concept of such consciousness-transcending things in themselves already contains an internal contradiction. In the assumption that we ourselves, not as physical beings but as spirits or minds, produce the ideas of sense in our consciousness, suggests a possible new answer to the question of these indisputably existent ideas. In fact, almost ever since Berkeley's doctrine has been known, it has been identified with subjective idealism of this kind.[34] This is however not the place for a detailed discussion of this mainstream interpretation.[35]

---

[32] Cf. footnote 13. Berkeley need not necessarily be understood as saying he denies the existence of matter (molecules, atoms etc.), but rather that he argues against the reality of the complete "otherness" of the spirit.

[33] The "master argument" has been interestingly analyzed and criticized by John L. Mackie, following Arthur N. Prior in using symbolic logic, in: Mackie, *Problems from Locke*, Oxford 1976, p. 53 f.

[34] Specific references will not be quoted here as almost all authors hold this position (with the important exception of A. A. Luce and T. E. Jessop).

[35] A discussion can be found for instance in: Aston A. Luce, *Berkeley's Immaterialism*, New York 1964².

Berkeley differentiates clearly between two types of ideas of sense. The first type comprises strong, lively and distinct ones, that "[...] have likewise a steadiness, order, and coherence, and are not excited at random".[36] The other type of ideas is not only significantly less clear, stable and ordered, it is also under my own control. I can assume that the latter, the "ideas of imagination" as they are being produced by me, exist only in my private world (this assumption has been confirmed in discussions about these matters with other people, whom I consider to be different - embodied - minds). However in the case of the former types, the "ideas of sense", I cannot assume in all modesty and reasonableness the same "privacy" and self-production to be true. These ideas of sense show such wonderful order, such reliability in their re-occurrence, they reveal such wisdom and foresight in their continuity, that I cannot conceive that they could have been produced by me or by one of my fellow creatures who seemingly are as "imperfect" as I am.

The unquestionable difference between the two types of ideas of sense demand an explanation. Obviously, the mind which produced the unequally more vivid, clearer and more durable ideas of sense, must be unequally stronger, clearer and more durable than the human mind. But before this discussion of Berkeley's proof of the existence of God is brought to a close, one further question should at least be posed: the question of what Berkeley understands by a finite or "limited mind", and, how he conceives our knowledge about it.

If we do not know what a finite mind is, what it is capable of or what it knows, then we also have no knowledge of why such a mind should not be able to produce the "strong" ideas of sense. What does Berkeley therefore have to say about those finite or creature's minds, that we ourselves are? If we ask ourselves this question (we will come back to it in Chapter V) while studying Berkeley's writings, the answer will be disappointing at first. We would have to join J.O. Urmson in saying:

> There is surprisingly little said about *spirits* and their nature in either the *Principles* or the *Dialogues*. Why this is so is unclear. In the private notebooks Berkeley wrote: 'Mem. Carefully to omit defining of person, or making much mention of it' (C 713).[37]

G. Pitcher goes beyond merely giving a factual statement. He expects Berkeley's philosophy to tell us "what the nature of that kind of substance is" and continues: "[...] Berkeley must of course have a position on this matter, for minds,

---

[36] Ayers (Ed.), p. 85 f. (*Priniples*, § 30).
[37] James O. Urmson, *Berkeley*, Oxford 1983, p. 58.

after all, are in his system the basic kind of thing that exists".[38] Pitcher can speak of the mind as the basic entity of Berkeley's philosophy because the underlying thought of this philosophy is that a relationship to "the self" exists always in everything I perceive, think etc.: it is **me** who perceives etc. (and so for all "minds"). The self represents the starting point of Berkeley's philosophy. And is Pitcher not perfectly right in expecting to hear something from Berkeley about this starting point? Obviously, he is: and there are actually - if somewhat hidden - references to it in Berkeley's writings. According to these "hints", the philosopher seems to have been of the opinion that **a kind of intuitive knowledge does exist about the self,** which somehow is pure activity and which cannot be developed into an idea. As we can see especially from his philosophy of language and the theory of meaning, which emerges from it [39], Berkeley obviously believed that it was not easy to speak meaningfully about this self and this connected intuitively experienced knowledge.

A first remark about this kind of knowledge appears in the *Philosophical Commentaries*[40] and is worded more precisely in the *Dialogues*.[41] There we read[42] that the self knows itself to be an intellectual active principle that perceives, recognizes, desires and works with ideas: "However I am not conscious in a similar way of either the existence or of the substance of matter". Berkeley protests against the well known reproach, recently repeated by A. Kulenkampff, that according to his own principles, Berkeley has to deny both the existence of material and spiritual substances.[43] But according to Berkeley everyone evidently knows about himself or herself **through reflexion.**[44] Thus, Berkeley believes that the self can somehow become a content of consciousness (if not as "element" or "fact among facts" of the consciousness), although he is also convinced that we are unable to produce any (distinct) "idea" about ourselves.[45] It is this intuitive knowledge about ourselves that teaches us our limitations and lets us understand clearly: we are not the cause of the strong ideas of sense and their totality, i.e. nature, nor are we the mastermind of the wonderful order to be found there (but nevertheless we are real minor or secondary causes).

---

[38] George Pitcher, *Berkeley*, London/Boston 1984², p. 203.
[39] Cf. in particular Berkeley's "Introduction" to the *Principles*, in: Ayers (Ed.), pp. 65-76.
[40] Cf. Ayers (Ed.), p. 305 (*Philosophical Commentaries*, No. 563).
[41] Cf. *Three Dialogues between Hylas and Philonous*, London 1713¹·, in: Ayers (Ed.), p. 135-207).
[42] Ayers (Ed.), p. 185, (Third Dialogue); in: Luce and Jessop (Eds.), p.234.
[43] Cf. Kulenkampff,. op. cit., p. 143. We will come back to this question in our last Chapter V, too.
[44] Ayers (Ed.), p. 184 (Third Dialogue).
[45] Ayers (Ed.), p. 124 (*Principles*, § 148); cf. our Chapter V for a more thoroughgoing discussion of Berkeley's theory of the mind.

I.4. Conclusion: There must be an intellectual being who is superior to us, who creates the ideas of sense, and in whom these ideas exist permanently: God

This suggests the conclusion - mindful of all the reflections of this first chapter - that the ideas of sense, which we perceive, are produced by a spirit significantly, if not infinitely, superior to our own. It also suggests that the corporeal (real) things exist in that spirit as they are nothing but collections of ideas. The common name for this very superior spiritual creator and sustainer is GOD. Having reached this conclusion, we are, according to Berkeley's opinion, not behaving unusually "metaphysical", but rather in an everyday common-sense manner: we would also infer the existence of **finite** minds in the same way:

> A human spirit or person is not perceived by sense, as not being an idea; when therefore we see the colour, size, figure, and motions of a man, we perceive only certain sensations or ideas excited in our own minds: and these being exhibited to our view in sundry distinct collections, serve to mark out unto us the existence of finite and created spirits like ourselves. Hence it is plain, we do not see a man, if by *man* is meant that which lives, moves, perceives and thinks as we do: but only such a certain collection of ideas, as directs us to think there is a distinct principle of thought and motion like to ourselves, accompanying and represented by it. And after the same manner we see God [...][46].

Berkeley suggests in the same text that the conclusion about the existence of other minds is not an imperative or necessary one (we are only "led to believe" by certain conceptual complexes that there are minds similar to our own).[47] The conclusion about the existence of God is indeed not an absolutely certain one as in mathematics, but (at least according to Berkeley) a very natural one, because the matter corresponds completely with our knowledge of other people's minds:

---

[46] Ayers (Ed.), p. 124 (*Principles*, § 148).

[47] Thus Berkeley did not combine his proof of the existence of God with any exaggerated hopes of a cogent or analytically necessary conclusion as in the models of the formal sciences. And this rightly so, as we can already read the following remark in the works of Aristotle: "We shall have to be satisfied with the degree of certainty, which is possibly given the material in questions. For we must not demand the same precision in every question, just as we wouldn't expect the same precision in the works of all crafts." (*Nicomachean Ethics*, I , 1094b, 11-13. Cf Wittgenstein's famous remark: "**Ein Ideal der Genauigkeit** gibt es nicht.").

[...] all the difference is, that whereas some one finite and narrow assemblage of ideas denotes a particular human mind, whithersoever we direct our view, we do at all times and in all places perceive manifest tokens of the divinity: everything we see, hear, feel, or any wise perceive by sense, being a sign or effect of the Power of God; [48]

A little later in paragraph 151 [49] Berkeley concludes his "proof" of the existence of God in the *Principles* with the following words:

> But though God conceal himself from the eyes of the *sensual* and the *lazy*, who will not be at the least expense of thought; yet to an unbiased and attentive mind, nothing can be more plainly legible, than the intimate presence of an *all-wise Spirit*, who fashions, regulates, and sustains the whole system of beings.

---

[48] Ayers (Ed.), p. 124 (*Principles,* § 148).
[49] Ayers (Ed.), p. 125.

II. The Theory of Objects (*Dialogues*)

II.0. Preliminary Remarks

Being precise, we have to admit that **the** definite written proof of the existence of God cannot be found with Berkeley. But there are differing "proofs" offered in his various writings. One argumentation is presented in the *Essay Towards a New Theory of Vision* (very similar but not identical: the *Theory of Vision Vindicated ... and Explained*, and *Alciphron: Part IV)* another - we know it already - can be found in the *Principles of Human Knowledge*. The *Three Dialogues between Hylas and Philonous* contain yet a further version, just as *De motu*, the early work *Philosophical Commentaries* and *Siris*, the work written in old age, do.

In expressing ourselves so differentiatedly we may be acting correctly, but there is the danger that by doing so we may - to use a German idiom - be reproached for "not seeing the forrest for of the trees". Obviously, these apparently separate proofs of the existence of God in Berkeley's writings **do** belong together and more or less are variations on a certain theme. Their common backbone is the argument developed in the *Principles* as discussed in the previous chapter. Of course, any thoroughgoing discussion of Bishop Berkeley's philosophical theology has to take these other argumentations into account, too. However, they should be regarded as supplements to his proof rather than revisions of it. It must also be noted that at least some of his proofs of the existence of God seem to be very inconclusive if regarded *prima facie* and taken out of the larger context. An example derived from the *Three Dialogues*[50], which we shall study in closer detail in this chapter, will illustrate this point clearly:

> Philonous: [...] *sensible things do really exist: and if they really exist, they are necessarily perceived by an infinite mind: therefore there is an infinite mind, or God*. This furnishes you with a direct and immediate demonstration, from a most evident principle, of the *being of a God* [...] that the sensible world is that which we perceive by our several senses; and that nothing is perceived by the senses beside ideas; and that no idea or archetype of an idea can exist otherwise than in a mind. You may now, without any laborious search into the sciences, without any subtlety of reason, or tedious length of discourse, oppose and baffle the most strenuous advocate for atheism.[51]

The *Three Dialogues* were published in 1713, three years after the *Principles* that had been completely misunderstood and unanimously rejected. According to his

---

[50] Cf. Ayers (Ed.), pp. 129-207.
[51] Ayers (Ed.), p. 168 f. (Second Dialogue).

own comments in the preface of this more popular postscript to his main work, Berkeley wanted to present his fundamental ideas once more "in the most easy and familiar manner" and to show them in a new light (the *Three Dialogues* are thus related to the *Principles* in the same way as Kant's *Prolegomena* is to the *Critique of Pure Reason*). Berkeley hoped here amongst other things to contribute towards bringing natural religion back "into regular systems, as artfully disposed and clearly connected as those of some other sciences."[52] Obviously, we are not just reading the outlines of a (rational theological) system of natural religion into Bishop Berkeley's works. They are actually there.

This "system" is discussed in the *Dialogues* above all with regard to the theory of objects: sensible objects or corporeal objects respectively do exist, but the existence of an infinite spirit is a prerequisite or necessary condition for their existence. Looking at the argument of the *Three Dialogues*, which is of particular interest for us, we can reconstruct it as follows:

1) The secondary qualities of a body exist only in the mind.
2) The primary qualities of a body are essentially the same as the secondary qualities.
3) A body does not consist of any additional "material substance" other than its perceptible qualities.
4) "Conclusion": A body is nothing but an isolated bundle of perceptible qualities (created to make life possible).

Let us begin with the explanation of these theses and the relevant arguments from the texts **in the spirit** of Berkeley's philosophy. We will also see that this argumentation gives his proof of the existence of God essential further support.

II.1. The secondary qualities of a body exist only in the mind

The classification of the characteristics or qualities of any perceptible object into primary or secondary ones (sometimes even tertiary, e.g. in Locke's theory) is part of the basic theoretical inventory of every atomistic philosophy, and, with a certain amount of good will, can even be found in the philosophy of Democritus. Combined with the renaissance of classical atomism at the beginning of modern times it has become the main starting point for "corpuscularian" philosophies, i.e. for

---

[52] Ayers (Ed.), p. 1327.

all the important natural scientists and a great number of philosophers (as can be shown in the works of Galileo, Newton, Boyle, Descartes, Gassendi, Hobbes, Locke and many others). Although the wording and the classification of the characteristics into two (or three) categories may differ slightly from author to author, they all seem to agree on the following basic assumptions:

All perceptible bodies are composed of minute corpuscles or atoms which can neither be divided further nor perceived individually. Bodies and corpuscles are similar to each other in their **primary** characteristics. These are - for the convenience of modern mathematised physics and chemistry - quantifiable. Examples of such primary qualities are: length, width and height ("extension"), weight and velocity. They differ from **secondary** not immediately quantifiable qualitiy characteristics such as individually experienced warmth and coldness, softness and hardness, sound, smell and taste. These "phenomena" exist only in the minds of people and some animals, each being caused by the "things in themselves" and their primary qualities. In these things we attribute the secondary characteristics to the configurations and forces of the corpuscles and their material qualities (shape, solidity etc.). The secondary qualities (which seem as such to be irrelevant for the exact sciences) have been raised - so to speak - to a second stage, to a metaphysical ("extensionless") place known as the consciousness. There they manage to keep alive, having, if we regard them as exact scientists, a truly shadowy existence as a kind of collective illusion of certain living organisms.

Berkeley would at least raise some interesting objections to the radical differentiation of the characteristics of objects into "real" and "apparent" qualities. Here he thinks he agrees with common sense, which we have to understand as a general (pre-or extra-scientific) human way of looking at things that does not allow the establishment of any essential differences, e.g. between the globular form and the green colour of a melon.

At a later date Henri Bergson states in the preface to his major work *Matière et Mémoire*:

> Un grand progrès fut réalisé en philosophie le jour où Berkeley établit, contre les 'mechanical philosophers', que les qualités secondaires de la matière avaient au moins autant de réalité que les qualités primaires. [53]

Berkeley's return to common sense may strike us as paradoxical at first, but he considered it the only feasible way. The direct way would be to prove that the green colour of a melon is just as much an independent, apparently solid and real quality, as

---

[53] Henri Bergson, *Oeuvres*, op. cit., p. 162.

is its round shape: that is to say that all qualities of objects have nothing to do with consciousness or mind.

But Berkeley would consider such reasoning not only to be demonstrably naive but also to conflict with his fundamental philosophical and religious convictions. According to them all objects and their qualities are "known" by God and owe therefore even their very existence to **this** consciousness.

Thus, only an indirect way of the reassimilation of primary and secondary qualities is left open. This has to take into account that **both** exist essentially in the same way in a conscious "mind", although it is completely independent from the consciousness of any human or animal (living creature). Thus, e.g. the melon's green colour is just as manifestly **ideal and real together** as its form and weight.

However, for this purpose and in contrast to the first assumption, form and weight have to be proved to be dependent on the consciousness and the mind as well as the colour. After this has been accomplished, the idea demands that the creaturely concept of consciousness, in the narrow sense, is replaced by a wider "creative" concept of the divine mind.

The last sentence of the Three Dialogues is totally in keeping with this idea: "[...] the same principles which at first view lead to **scepticism**, pursued to a certain point, bring men back to common sense." [54]

Berkeley's *Dialogue* arguments, substantiating the idea that the secondary qualities are dependent on consciousness, are evidently orientated on the corresponding exposition in John Locke's *Essay Concerning Human Understanding*. [55]

Both philosophers consider the discussion about the heat of fire and warmth as a particularly promising starting point for their aims: just as the pain we experience when a needle is stuck into our body, is not part of the object itself, we cannot reasonably assume that a fire contains the very unpleasant idea of painfully burning heat. In the same way, it makes sense to assume that a fire does not contain the slightly unpleasant idea of "ordinary" heat. If this is true, it does not contain the pleasant sensation of warmth either.

The objection that aversion to heat and desire for warmth are only the disagreeable or agreeable subjective effects of different things respectively their qualities, is rejected with the following remark: in each case only simple sensations are immediately experienced, whereas sensations that are not perceptible (i.e. pure qualities that are neither agreeable nor disagreeable), are not even mentioned.

---

[54] Ayers (Ed.), p. 207..
[55] Numerous editions. Cf. esp. the Second Book, Chapter 8.

Therefore, the question is: where do these simple and sensually real sensations exist? The answer must inevitably be: "in the mind, not in the fire." This thesis is substantiated further by the accompanying (mental or thought-) experiment of the two hands of varying temperatures. We have to imagine that one hand has been warmed while the other has been cooled, and that they both are plunged into luke-warm water. The water will feel cold to the warm hand and warm to the cool hand. Assuming the well-known Aristotelian principle that contradictory predicates cannot be applied to one and the same object (in this case water), it follows that the coldness and the warmth are not in the water itself. At this point the objection may be raised that a thermometer would indicate a certain water temperature. However, John Locke who is the spiritus rector of this thought experiment ("Gedankenexperiment"), could respond to this objection by referring to the movement of the "water corpuscles" (H_2O molecules) that have an effect on (intermediary: glass resp. Si molecules) the mercury corpuscles (Hg molecules) in the thermometer. Movements such as these could be accepted without leading to the conclusion that secondary qualities such as perceptible warmth or coldness are inherent in the water itself.

Berkeley follows up this argument by discussing the secondary qualities of taste, smell, sound and (visual) colour in turn. He makes short work of the transposition of both, the pleasant taste of sugar and the bad smell of excrement in our consciousness: such desirable or undesirable sensations (and every sensation has at least **some** element markedly desirable or undesirable) are not to be found in materially insensitive bodies. With regard to sounds he discusses a differentiation of the concept of "sound". He distinguishes between the usual meaning of the word, namely as "sound sensation" for the sounds as we can hear them, and sound in the "real and philosophical" sense, namely as a particular wave-movement of the air. Berkeley tries to develop the idea of the "philosophical" meaning of sound to a point of absurdity by asking with which sense we can detect movements. The answer is: not with the sense of hearing, but usually with the visual and tactile senses. This reasoning would produce the extraordinary conclusion that "real" sounds are never heard, whereas they could possibly be **seen** and **felt** ... His consideration of colours and their ontological "location" (in the "realm" of the consciousness) is the most detailed of his expositions on this subject. Berkeley achieves his aim of presenting the thesis that colours are purely elements of the consciousness through the intermediary conclusion "that there is no such thing as colour really inherent in external bodies, but that it is altogether in the light".[56]

One reason why it is not possible for inherent body colours or colours as material corporeal surfaces to exist in themselves, lies in the impossibility of defining

---

[56] Ayers (Ed.), p. 147.

the true colours of a material body. If we look at a church tower from a distance for example (it is not exactly Berkeley's example), it seems to be of a hazy-blue colour. As we approach it, the colour appears to change to grey. If we stand very close to it, we see possibly that it is built of stones varying slightly in their colouring (predominately white, brown, ochre, black etc). However, if we examined a minute piece of one of these stones (especially if containing quartz and put under the microscope), we would see nearly all the colours of the rainbow. What is the real colour of the church tower then? The problem here is, that the question asked has been wrongly formulated because it was based on a mistaken initial assumption. Colours are simply **not** surfaces of church towers or any other material bodies. Colours are, to use Goethe's fine words, "Taten und Leiden des Lichts". Goethe shares **this** fundamental conviction with Newton as indeed Berkeley has also done **up to now**. The point where Berkeley's view begins to deviate from Newton's is where he is not willing to agree that coloured light is "a corporeal substance outside the mind". Colour as a modification of light is (in the context of a scientific perspective) an acceptable conception for Berkeley (cf. our Chapter IV). But "true" light is perceptible and not a light which can principally not be perceived, and which consists of some "thin fluid substance [...] whose minute particles [are] being agitated with a brisk motion and in various manners reflected from the different surfaces of outward objects to the eyes".[57] Light, when defined in this "real or philosophical" (Newtonian) sense, could neither contain colour sensations nor produce them in the mind. Here, once again, Philonous (the "friend of the nous" and Berkeley's mouthpiece in the *Three Dialogues*) tries (successfully) to bewilder his materialistically-minded opponent Hylas ("matter") with an *argumentum ad absurdum*:

> *Philonous:* [...] only I would advise you to bethink yourself, whether considering the inquiry we are upon, it be prudent for you to affirm, *the red and blue which we see are not real colours, but certain unknown motions and figures which no man ever did or can see, are truly so.* Are not these shocking notions, and are not they subject to as many ridiculous inferences, as those you were obliged to renounce before in the case of sounds?
>
> *Hylas*: I frankly own, Philonous, that it is in vain to stand out any longer. Colours, sounds, tastes, in a word, all those termed *secondary qualities*, have certainly no existence without the mind.[58]

---

[57] Ayers (Ed.), p. 148.
[58] Ayers (Ed.), p. 148.

II.2. The primary qualities of a body are essentially the same as the secondary qualities

According to Locke, the major characteristics of the primary qualities are their quantifiability and their close affinity with the human tactile sense, as well as their absoluteness (their "non-relativity" to the observer) and a certain "veridical" character which prevents them from being misrepresented while being perceived. Even if we are unaware of Berkeley's arguments, these criteria may seem a little odd. Why should a quality that can be measured and calculated, be in any way more "real" than one that is not quantifiable?

Does not a piece of metaphysical Platonism [59] or even mystical Pythagorism come to the light here? This peculiarity which consists of awarding the tactile sense a special status as the "reality sense" (strangely enough the primary qualities are all tactile), may strengthen the suspicion that - in a broader sense - irrationalism is somehow secretly at work here. The bread we can also touch is of course more nutritious than the one we can merely see; the arrow which we feel is more dangerous than the one we merely hear. However, the question may be repeated: can the question of the reality of a quality be unreflectively decided by considering how important that quality is for human life and biological survival?

As far as the alleged absoluteness of the primary qualities is concerned, the following simple "thought experiment" may arouse a certain amount of doubt: a shiny green melon appears darker by daylight when held close to the eye than when held at an arm's length ("secondary quality relativity"). And yet, in the latter case it will undoubtedly seem **heavier**, too. So what about the absoluteness of the primary quality of weight here? We might calmly answer this by saying that only the apparent weight has changed, whereas the absolute weight (e.g. 5 pounds) remains in any case. The objection looks disputable. Firstly the (abridged) statement "5 pounds", that seems to be so absolute, possibly only conceals a relational predicate ("the melon weighs as much as five iron weights of a certain size" or "... as much as ten oranges" or ...). And secondly the question of the colour quality "green" could be answered along similar lines: "only the apparent colour seems to change, the absolute colour remains having a wave lenght of 520 millimicron".

But still we are left with Locke's argument that water can at one and the same time give the impression of warmth to the one hand and of coldness to the other. This does **not** apply with regard to primary qualities as Locke maintained when writing about the impressions given to both hands when feeling shapes, "which yet figure never does, that never producing the idea of a square by one hand, which has

---

[59] Galileo was undoubtedly a Platonist in this sense.

produced the idea of a globe by the other".[60] In reality (pace Locke) the tactile sense can also be misled. This happens often enough in dreams, but can also occur when we are only half asleep. We can then feel for instance that we are holding something in our arms or hands that disappears completely right at the moment of waking up properly. But even when wide awake it is still possible for our senses to be deceived through what our hands feel:

> One of the first observations of this kind was made by James Gibson in the early 1930s. In the course of conducting an experiment on the effect of continued exposure to a visually curved line, Gibson required the observers to look at a perfect straight rod through a wedge prism, which rendered its image curved. He reported that, when objects were allowed to run their hands along the rod, which should have provided haptic information that the rod was straight, it neither looked straight nor felt straight. In fact, it felt curved, just the way it looked.[61]

One of Berkeley's main arguments against the thesis that primary qualities are elements of being, while secondary qualities are elements of consciousness, is that speaking of primary ideas such as "extension" is nothing more than empty juggling with abstract concepts, unless it is underlayed by perception or imagination. Reflecion shows that both sorts of qualities are always connected indissolubly. An object we can feel to be extended, is also coloured, and all impressions of colour prove to be connected with extension, most with an object to be felt. This main argument is supplemented by reference to the relativity of observation as regards secondary **and** primary characteristics: Changing the distance between the observer and the observed object not only influences the perception of colour and smell and so forth (e.g. of a rose), but also the impression of its size and form etc. Locke's famous experiment with the two hands and the different temperature sensations can also be carried out with the primary quality of size: it is not only possible (Berkeley discovered) to perceive one and the same thing at the same time as being both, hot and cold, but also as being both, large and small. This is for instance the case when we look at an object through a microscope with one eye only, using the other eye naked.

Furthermore, the experienced weight of an object and its solidity (another primary quality), i.e. the degree to which the object proves resistant against any attempt of penetration, depends on the type and strength of the experiencing and

---

[60] *Essay*, Book 2, Chap. 8, Sect. 21 (*The Works of John Locke,* in 10 Volumes, London 1823, Vol. 1, p. 125).
[61] Irvin Rock, *Perception*, New York 1984, p. 137.

acting subject respectively. Non-perceptible velocity is an empty abstract idea and perceptible velocity changes as quickly as the sequence of images in the perceiving mind changes. Here Berkeley is obviously thinking of the experience of mail-coach passengers (or in more modern terms - railway passengers), who manage to change their own impression of speed. When looking out of the window, objects can voluntarily be made to look as if they were flashing by slowlier. This happens when passengers at first move their eyes very quickly with the direction of their own movement while later their gaze remains on an outside object until it disappears from their field of vision. The feeling of speed also changes, depending on how near or far the object outside is from the observer. Once we have accepted that certain "qualities of objects" such as heat, smell or colour, only really exist in the minds of the perceivers, a clear-cut separation of object and subject, of being and mind is (according to Berkeley) no longer possible.

Then there is no holding back and all qualities flow - at least in **one** aspect of their existence - into the mind as their legitimate philosophical location: here "in one aspect of their existence" means that it is still possible in any case to distinguish between these (primary or secondary) qualities with regard to whether they are merely perceived ("apparent" or "phenomenal") aspects or whether they are actually existent ("real") aspects ("real" could mean here: functioning in a scientific theory - more of this again in our Chapter IV). Thus, in the example previously mentioned, the merely apparent (perceptible) speed of the coach can be distinguished from the existent (imperceptible) speed. This differentiation should be left open for the time being, although some criticism has already been attempted. It can be noted that all perceptible qualities of an object are connected with the consciousness of the perceiver, or more strictly speaking, with his animated body. The perceiver himself or herself regards this connection as indissoluble. He or she is not able to distinguish in his or her own experience between colour sensations and real colours, nor between the sensation of speed and the "actual" speed. Thus, if we take the **object actually perceived** into consideration, the differentiation between primary and secondary qualities proves untenable. However, this does not lead to the conclusion that a differentiation between qualities must be of no use at all. Such a differentiation could be accompanied by two differing object concepts: object 1 as the sum of all its perceptible elements and qualities, the object of the "world of life" ("Lebenswelt"), and object 2 as the sum of all the imperceptible elements and qualities, the object of physical (and chemical etc.) theory ("world of science").

Husserl's discussion in *Ideen zu einer reinen Phänomenologie* may throw some light on this matter. The idea that it is possible to distinguish between primary and secondary qualities cannot reasonably be interpreted in the sense that we are left with the "real" object and its primary qualities if we take away the secondary qualities:

So verstanden hätte ja der alte Berkeleysche Einwand recht, daß die Ausdehnung, dieser Wesenskern der Körperlichkeit und aller primären Qualitäten, undenkbar sei ohne sekundäre. Vielmehr *der ganze Wesensgehalt des wahrgenommenen Dinges*, also das ganze in Leibhaftigkeit dastehende mit allen seinen Qualitäten und allen je wahrnehmbaren, ist *bloße Erscheinung*, und das *"wahre Ding" ist das der physikalischen Wissenschaft*. Wenn diese das gegebene Ding ausschließlich durch Begriffe wie Atome, Ionen, Energien usw. bestimmt und jedenfalls als raumerfüllende Vorgänge, deren einzige Charakteristika mathematische Ausdrücke sind, so meint sie *ein dem gesamten in Leibhaftigkeit dastehenden Dinginhalt Transzendentes.* So kann das Ding dann nicht einmal als im natürlichen Sinnenraum liegendes meinen; mit anderen Worten, ihr physikalischer Raum kann nicht der Raum der leibhaften Wahrnehmungswelt sein: sie verfiele ja sonst ebenfalls den Berkeleyschen Einwänden. [62]

The objection of Berkeley we are discussing here, claiming that a connection between the ideas of ("physical") extension and secondary qualities is necessary, runs like this: "that where the one exist [sic!] there necessarily the other exist [sic!] likewise."[63]

In this context the following statement is Berkeley's "final word" on the subject of the so-called essential difference between primary and secondary qualities:

> If it be allowed that no idea nor any thing like an idea can exist in an unperceiving substance, then surely it follows, that no figure or mode of extension, which we can either perceive or imagine, or have any idea of, can be really inherent in matter; not to mention the peculiar difficulty there must be, in conceiving a material substance, prior to and distinct from extension., to be the *substratum* of extension. [64]

The reason why there is a "peculiar difficulty" here, and the clarification of this difficulty that proves even more difficult when looked at closer, shall be the topic of the following section.

---

[62] Edmund Husserl, *Ideen zu einer reinen Phänomenologie und phänomenologischen Philosophie*, Erstes Buch, ed. Elisabeth Ströker, Vol. 5, Hamburg 1992, p. 82, §. 40.
[63] Ayers (Ed.), p. 153.
[64] Ayers (Ed.), p. 150.

II.3. A body does not consist of any additional "material substance" other than its perceptible qualities

It may seem as if Berkeley ought to have developed further systematic arguments here in order to substantiate his immaterialistic theory of objects.

Berkeley only raises two objections against speaking of real qualities (today: electromagnetic wave-particle oscillations as differences in colour, medium kinetic energy as "warmth" etc): one is a linguistic usage argument and the other a theoretical semantic argument. Neither is very convincing. According to the first argument it would sound very strange to hear someone say things such as "real sounds cannot be heard" or "real colours cannot be seen". Such an argument, appealing to a *façon de parler*, certainly is hardly plausible, particularly when attributed to Berkeley. In Paragraph 38 of the *Principles*, Berkeley himself admits that it would sound "harsh" if he said (what he must do) that we "eat and drink ideas, and are clothed with ideas". His second objection is closely related to his radical empirical theory of meaning whose foundation was laid already down in the *Philosophical Commentaries*. According to it linguistic expressions either fulfil syntactic (syncategorimatical) functions or have to represent ideas (as individual terms) in order to be (categorimatically) meaningful. Berkeley carefully qualified this statement later by admitting that some concepts such as will, soul, spirit etc. could be meaningful even though we may not be able to connect them to ideas. The results of intuitive self-perception (introspection) would then replace the missing ideas. A certain amount of meaning, adequate for many purposes, could also be derived somehow through the (quantitative and qualitative) expansion of these introspective experiences (that are difficult to verbalise), and through the words associated with them. Berkeley also is thinking of a possible transfer of meaning here, for example from a "human" to a "divine" mind. His theory of meaning is nevertheless in another way radically empirical. Unlike Locke's "conceptualist" version for instance, which he criticizes [65], he categorically rejects the use of "abstract general ideas" as meanings for general terms.

Berkeley argues that general ideas such as "**the** triangle" cannot exist because their characteristics contradict each other ("the" triangle would for instance have to be neither rectangular nor not rectangular, but also both together ...). Berkeley wants to replace these general ideas with the idea of a **particular** triangle that can be considered as representative for all triangles. [66]

---

[65] Cf. esp. the "Introduction" to the *Principles*, in Ayers (Ed.), pp. 65-76.

[66] Berkeley, other than Hume, does not continue by saying that we do not need to imagine a particular triangle every time we speak, hear or read the word "triangle". For Hume the

The Pythagoras theorem was not proved valid for all right-angled triangles only because the idea of **the** right-angled triangle had been focussed on and made use of. Was not the general validity rather a result of the fact that certain limitations, such as the equality or difference of the lengths of the catheters, or of the two angles of the hypotenuse etc., were **disregarded**? Thus, according to Berkeley, an individual idea may represent all its "similar" ideas, and the existence of similarities between ideas (and collections of ideas of sense, i.e. natural things) is simply a fact and not to be further queried.

This is not the place for an adequate criticism of the nominalist (empiricist) theory of meaning (which is not simply identical with Berkeley's). However, two critical comments which complement each other should be noted here: on the one hand, a single idea or an individual thing is not *per se* representative of its class, type or species. The condition of the fulfillment of such a paradigm function is the knowledge of what characterises this class (etc.) and what limits it, i.e. a **concept**. Thus, this "representation theory" assumes exactly that which should be explained by it and made expendable... On the other hand, "similarity", which together with "representation" is one of the two basic concepts of such nominalist theories, is a three-figure predicate, as opposed to the two-figure predicate that it might seem at first sight. In some respects all things in our universe are "similar" to all other things, but only certain things are similar to others **with respect to particular aspects**. That means: to speak meaningfully about similarity requires the prior knowledge of the **manner** in which similar objects are classified, A with B, C, etc. - Once again we have a somewhat abstract intellectual achievement we would have been glad to avoid. Looking at the matter this way, Locke is right against Berkeley and Hume[67]: if we assume that sentence elements, and not just whole sentences, are meaningful (but obviously this assumption is debatable), then we seem unable to avoid the postulate that abstract general ideas are the meaning of general terms.

Admittedly, Locke sometimes expounds this correct insight in a slightly awkward manner.[68] He gives the impression that the meaning of a concept has to be an abstract idea which is an intellectually stimulating, but vague picture or bundle of pictures which comes to consciousness "in a flash ". He would probably have done better to suggest the idea instead that such a concept consists of knowledge of how a sequence of ideas is produced in the mind according to a rule, together with

---

simple word "triangle" (as a sequence of sounds or letters) can take on a representative function; at any rate so after it has become an integral part of a person's language competence.

[67] Cf. David Hume, "A Treatise on Human Nature", Part 1, Sect. VII (*Of abstract Ideas*), in: Thomas G. Hill and Thomas H. Grose (Ed.), *The Philosophical Works of David Hume*, London 1986, Vol. 1, p. 325 ff.

[68] Cf. for example *Essay*, Book IV, Chapter 7, Section 9.

knowledge of how the word is to be used in accordance with the accepted conventions of speaking in a community of speakers.

This brings us to the conclusion that Berkeley's direct ("language-centered") objections to speaking of "real" qualities (as opposed to perceptible, "merely phenomenal" ones) - as connected with real substances - are indeed rather unsatisfactory. In fact he invested more time and effort in the formulation of an **indirect** objection himself which is based on the assumption that real qualities are dependent on the existence of real substance, i.e. matter: if it was possible to show that bodies can impossibly consist of (among other "things") any sort of "material substance" or "material substrate", then the postulate of the existence of material or real material qualities of these substances or substrata is superfluous. Briefly speaking, if we drop the concept of the material substance of an object, we also lose the concept of "real" qualities. What objection is being raised here to the first of these two concepts?

Berkeley wants to use the word "matter" in the way it was generally accepted by his contemporaries ("in the common current acceptation of the word"), defining it as "an extended, solid, moveable, unthinking, inactive substance".[69] He feels unhesitatingly certain that "thinking" cannot be caused by anything like "unthinking" matter. Obviously, this objection is based on the question whether it makes sense to postulate imperceptible qualities as well as perceptible, experiencable ones. How, for instance, is the transformation of an electromagnetic "wave" in a sensation of red (in the perceived colour red) possible? This transformation seems to be even more unlikely, even "absurd", if the brain is understood as being merely one of several objects of sense (namely if thereby the reality of the mind is denied).[70]

There is an additional difficulty. We cannot be sure that Berkeley himself was aware of it, but perhaps he was referring to it in the following statement: "can anything be plainer, than that we see them [colours, S. B.] on the objects?"[71] If real colour is a (complementary) electromagnetic wave-corpuscule ray, why do we see the colour clearly and visibly limited to the surface of the "coloured object", without having the least impression that the colour (just like the rays) reaches from this surface to our eyes?[72]

However, this difficulty is not discussed any further: other arguments are of greater significance for the philosopher. The most important of them is that a material

---

[69] Ayers (Ed.), p. 172.
[70] This topic has already been shortly discussed in the previous chapter. Cf. also Ayers (Ed.), p. 166 (*Dialogues*).
[71] Ayers (Ed.), p. 195.
[72] We know this feeling, but we only seldom experience it; e.g. when we are surrounded by mist or fog which is illuminated by coloured lights.

substance is not perceptible - more strictly speaking "principally imperceptible". In fact, Locke was, as a consequence of his own assumptions, forced to admit that the real (as opposed to the merely "nominal") material existence of each object is a pure X, an "I don't know what". Berkeley (and also Leibniz) taught that this thesis of matter being completely unknown and unfathomable, contained "dangerous seeds of atheism"; for it can no longer be precluded that the source of design and order in the world as well as the principle of the human minds originate in **matter itself**. For Berkeley, the consequence of this idea that we know absolutely nothing about the essence of the most common object in everyday life, is untenable in the first place because it is incompatible with common sense. (It is also superfluous. This because the concept of God - His omnipresent spirit - replaces the concept of matter very properly). But to repeat: the existence of objects of sense (and things in the "Lebenswelt") is thereby **not** necessarily denied although this is generally thought to be part of his immaterialistic ("idealist") theory.

> That the colours are really in the tulip which I see, is manifest. Neither can it be denied, that this tulip may exist independent of your mind or mine. [73]

> The question between the materialists and me is not, whether things have a real existence out of the mind of this or that person, but whether they have an absolute existence, distinct from being perceived by God, and exterior to all minds. [74]

He here only objects to the reality of a material substance, not to the reality of a cosmos existing independent of human (and animal) consciousness. The claim that such a reality exists, represents even **one important premise** of the immaterialistic proof of God's existence. For, if the following idea that the destruction of all conscious living creatures on earth means that the whole cosmos would be annihilated, is conceivable and believable, then there would be absolutely no need for bringing the divine spirit "into play": but of course, for Berkeley as for "common sense" this idea is not believable. Thus, Berkeley (here only?) is a decidedly ontological realist with respect to the "external world" and this realism is already based in the centre of his proof of God's existence; however his realism is no materialism.

The acceptance of immaterialism he fancied to be useful to religion, whereas the acceptance of materialism for him is of use directly to scepticism only and indirectly to atheism. In line with these "pragmatic" arguments is a further one, which has also

---

[73] Ayers (Ed.), p. 154.
[74] Ayers (Ed.), p. 186. Cf. also ibid., p. 87 (*Principles*, § 35).

already been discussed and which Berkeley himself emphasized especially, his "master argument".[75]

The following arguments against material substance can also be found, although these are of secondary importance to the marked ones discussed above. They run as follows: "particularly for a christian" the postulate of matter produces (*firstly*) a strange hypothesis duplication. From the very beginning the perceptible world has existed in God's thoughts, so why do we need to look for a second persisting *substratum* in the form of matter? *Secondly* the connection of an imperceptible material substance with perceptible qualities is completely inconceivable and unbelievable. *Thirdly* a causal conclusion from the domain of experience into a (maintained) unknown domain of matter, i.e. a **true world** of science, is inadmissible. Here again Husserl's enlightening remarks on Berkeley's philosophy:

> Mit seinem genialen Blick erschaut er auch den Widersinn der Locke'schen Lehre von der äußeren Existenz und den eines jeden Kausalschlusses, der in das Transzendent-Physische führt. Das innere Wahrnehmungsbild des äußeren Dinges soll nach Locke ein assoziativer Komplex von Sinnesdaten der verschiedenen Sinne sein, die von den äußeren Naturdingen kausal herstammen. Der Geist kann [könne S. B.] nicht anders, als solch einem assoziativen Komplex ein *Je ne sais quoi* als "Träger" unterlegen, wobei ein Kausalschluß von der Wirkung auf eine transzendente Ursache eine Rolle spielt. Vortrefflich wendet Berkeley ein, ein solcher Schluß sei unausweisbar und unausdenkbar.[76]

He writes in another place on the same subject:

> Widersinnigerweise verknüpft man also Sinnendinge und physikalische Dinge durch *Kausalität*. [...] Die Kausalität, die prinzipiell in den Zusammenhang der konstituierten intentionalen Welt hineingehört und nur in ihr einen Sinn hat, macht man nun [...] zu einem mystischen Bande zwischen dem "objektiven" physikalischen Sein und dem "subjektiven", in der unmittelbaren Erfahrung erscheinenden Sein - dem "bloß subjektiven" Sinnendinge mit den "sekundären Qualitäten [...][77]

---

[75] Cf. the *Dialogues*, p. 158. Cf. also André Gallois "Berkeley's Master Argument", *Philosophical Review* 83 (1979), p. 55 ff.

[76] Edmund Husserl, *Erste Philosophie* (Ed. Elisabeth Ströker), *Gesammelte Schriften*, Vol. 6, p. 113 f.
To quote Berkeley himself: "[...] I have no reason for believing the existence of matter. I have no immediate intuition thereof: neither can I mediately from my sensations, ideas, notions, actions or passions, infer an unthinking, unperceiving, inactive substance, either by probable deduction, or necessary consequence." Ayers (Ed.), p. 184.

[77] Ibid., p. 114.

II.4. A body is nothing but an isolated bundle of perceptible qualities - created to make life possible

The reconstruction of Berkeley's theory of objects as presented in the *Three Dialogues* is now almost complete. The two favourite philosophical distinctions between (firstly) material substratum and perceivable qualities and (secondly) between primary and secondary qualities - distinctions which common sense hardly if at all acknowledges - are theoretically ill-conceived and have been rejected as well because their effects are even "dangerous". At first sight it of course would seem **that the dependency on consciousness of the whole sensually perceptible object** is being emphasized as opposed to common sense.[78] B u t :

> Philonous: I do not pretend to be a setter-up of *new notions*. My endeavours tend only to unite and place in a clearer light that truth, which was before shared between the vulgar and the philosophers: the former being of opinion, that *those things they immediately perceive are the real things*; and the latter, that *the things immediately perceived, are ideas which exist only in the mind*. Which two notions put together do in effect constitute the substance of what I advance.[79]

According to Philonous-Berkeley, an object is "represented" in our human minds **basically as perceivable without any principally unperceivable** remnants. These objects fill a certain domain or section of the infinite amount of ideas of the eternal and ever present (thinking) divine mind. This purely active mind influences our minds through its ideas. However, the way in which divine ideas are classified and organised (all expressions *cum grano salis*), is according to Berkeley the work of man. The utmost standard or criterion of the organisation of certain ideas of sense into bundles of ideas, named "objects" or "bodies", is not god or human abstract theory but life itself. For, all living beings were given senses for their preservation and well-being[80], and the words "were framed by the vulgar, merely for convenience and dispatch in the common actions of life, without any regard to speculation."[81]

> But in case every variation [of ideas] was thought sufficient: to constitute a new kind or individual, the endless number or confusion of names would

---

[78] This impression changes as soon as it is clear that Berkeley uses the expression "consciousness-dependency" to signify the dependence on God rather than on humans. This point of view has obviously been consistent with the views of Berkeley's (Irish) contemporaries: "But then to a Christian it cannot surely be shocking to say, the real tree existing without his mind is truly known and comprehended by (that is *exists in*) the infinite mind of God." Ayers (Ed.), p. 186.
[79] Ayers (Ed.), p. 207.
[80] Cf. Ayers (Ed.), p. 149.
[81] Ayers (Ed.), p. 194.

render language impracticable. Therefore to avoid this as well as other inconveniences which are obvious upon a little thought, men combine together several ideas, apprehended by divers senses, or by the same sense at different times, or in different circumstances, but observed however to have some connexion in nature, either with respect to co-existence or succession; all which they refer to one name, and consider as one thing.[82]

---

[82] Ayers (Ed.), p. 194.

III. The Argument for a Divine Providence (*New Theory*)
III.0. Preliminary remarks

The development of philosophy towards the reflected knowledge of the world by paying close attention to human mind and intellectual capacity, was led by René Descartes. John Locke's *Essay Concerning Human Understanding*"[83], is a partially independent continuation of this development. As in the works of Malebranche[84], Locke's writings are also taking into account that all knowledge is based on the specifically human cognitive capacity, which means that propositions about external material objects can no longer be regarded as knowledge of the "things in themselves". That Locke does take due notice of this fact can be seen in his extensive use of the word "idea", the etymon of his philosophy. Wherefrom, does Locke ask, gets the human mind the material for its activity in the first place? "My answer to this is a single word - experience."[85] According to Berkeley, there is a double source of human knowledge, from external (and internal) perception, and through reflection on our own intellectual operations ("intuition").

For Descartes (who also knows this "knowledge by intuition") the realm of material things was totally different from the realm of the mind and the essence of the material world lay in its extension: as we can define this extension mathematically, we should be able to fully understand the material, i.e. extended world. In Locke's writings the extension looses the importance it had held in Descartes' object theory - extension is just **one** of the primary or real-thing predicates. However, there remains the idea of the existence of an extended material world radically independent of any kind of consciousness. According to Berkeley, such a world would lack (so to speak) "the ability of self-revelation", i.e. the openness for knowledge in general. Just as this principal openness, our ability of putting the "world" into mathematical terms ought not simply to be accepted as being self-evident, but the "fitting" of mathematics to reality is rather an asthonishing fact.

Whenever the word "extension" is uttered, we (as philosophers) cannot disregard the concept of extension itself. We think that this fundamental thought of

---

[83] John Locke, *Essay Concerning Human Understanding*, London 1690.
[84] Cf. Nicholas Malebranche, *Recherches de la Vérité*, Paris 1674/75 (Vol. 2, *Ecclairissements*, 1678).
Malebranche's influence on Berkeley has received different interpretations. Cf. Arthur A. Luce, *Berkeley and Malebranche: A Study in the Origins of Berkeley's Thought*, Oxford 1967. Harry M. Bracken, *Berkeley*, London 1974, p. 18 goes to the extreme of claiming that, if he must be labelled at all, Berkeley might more accurately be called an Irish Cartesian (Malebrancheian), than a British empiricist.
[85] John Locke, *Essay*, Book II, Chapt. I, Sect. II.

Berkeley's can be illustrated by using even the simplest form of extension, the straight line. If we but "feel" from point to point, either with our finger, our eyes or with our imagination alone, we would not gain the impression of extension. This can only occur in a situation where the process of tactile, visual or mental traversing of the line of the previously traversed section is simultaneously remembered, and in turn associated with the actual movement. That is to say, that not only **movement** is a prerequisite for the concept of extension, but also **time**. However, we cannot even leave the matter here. We have rather to consider motion and duration as being joined in a kind of lasting and unifying (so to speak) **substantial point of consciousness**: "I wonder how men cannot see a truth so obvious, as that extension cannot exist without a thinking substance."[86] Whereas Locke regarded extension as an essential characteristic of matter, Descartes felt it was the very essence of such matter itself. But as we cannot even think of real abstract extension by itself (and apart from us conceptualizing "thinking substances") without there being an inconsistency with the preconditions for our concept of extension, it is (so Berkeley concludes) impossible to speak of this extension in such a naively realistic way.

As we have seen Berkeley thinks it necessary to add a constituent "X" to the concept of extension, and he speaks - in terms that are general (or vague) enough - of a "thinking substance" in order to express his thought: ideas have to be regarded as being connected with each other through an (unextended) unifying "point". The concept of this thinking substance logically precedes that of the extended matter. **Can thus any theory which uses matter as its basic explanatory principle be proven to be ill-conceived?** Here we are allowed to join up with Berkeley's original insight in a more general sense: if we call these theories "materialistic", we can understand his need of finding alternative theories which are not materialist but "immaterialist". - The philosopher's need here converges at the same time in an unconstrained way with his more personal need as a Christian apologist and bishop.

But now we are asked whether we can really accept the idea that the (extended) world could be held together inwardly by such a "limited" spirit as the human mind. This would at least be difficult to conceive, and thus we have found the intellectual ground for an argument for accepting the existence of an intellectual principle which is quite simply infinitely superior to that of human beings. We have called this "George Berkeley's argument for the existence of God" and given a detailed account of it particularly in our first chapter. However, the argument for the existence of such a cosmic spirit is itself insufficient for both, Berkeley's apologetic and ethical aims. He is concerned with proving a fact, or rather a being that is, or should be, of importance for the Christian religion and for everybodies life. This means that the

---

[86] Ayers (Ed.), p. 275 (*Philosophical Commentaries*, § 270).

plausibility of the idea of a **divine personality** has to be proven. Berkeley wants to demonstrate this by developing a special argument for divine providence (rather than divine "predestination", believing as he did in the freedom of the will).[87] Only if can be shown that a cosmic spirit wants to save us from harm and is also willing and able to do so, the goodness and wisdom, and finally also the personality of this being, would have been demonstrated.

III.1. Berkeley's thesis that visual ideas of sense are a language of God and a primary means of his providence

Berkeley's ideas about divine providence are clearly and comprehensively explained in his works *New Theory of Vision* (1709), *Theory of Vision ... Vindicated and Explained* (1733) and *Alciphron: or The Minute Philosopher* (1732).[88] Paul J. Olscamp has described the fundamental idea underlying this account, namely **that the visual world is a language of God which gives us information about the corporeal tactile world**, as being the "keystone to George Berkeley's ontology, epistemology and moral philosophy".[89] There may be a slight exaggeration here, but the idea of the "visual language of God" is undoubtedly of importance for Berkeley's philosophy. This is especially true for his philosophical writings in which he considers the tactile sense to be of particular importance. In connection with this remark we can divide Berkeley's main works into two groups. In the first group *(Principles of Human Knowledge* and the *Three Dialogues between Hylas and Philonous)* he treats all human senses alike in principle, whereas in the second group *(New Theory of Vision, Alciphron: or the Minute Philosopher* and the *Theory of Vision ... Vindicated and Explained)* he writes that the tactile sense differs from our other senses in that its perceptions or ideas **do not come directly** from God but are caused by a material world. It is **only** through the ideas of the tactile sense that we are made aware of a reality, or world, which God created long ago and which he keeps in existence by means of the laws of nature. All the senses are given equal treatment in the first group of works mentioned, but even here the tactile sense is clearly regarded as the most important sense as far as life and survival are concerned. But let us now turn to Berkeley's thesis that the visual ideas of sense represent a divine language.

---

[87] Cf. esp. *Alciphron: or the Minute Philosopher* (Eighth Dialogue), in: Arthur A. Luce and Thomas E. Jessop, *The Works of George Berkeley*, London 1948, Vol. III, 1950.
[88] Ayers (Ed.), *New Theory of Vision, pp. 1-59, The Theory of Vision ... Vindicated and Explained,* pp. 229-250; and *Alciphron* (see note above).
[89] Paul J. Olscamp, *The Moral Philosophy of George Berkeley*, The Hague 1970, p. 10.

For Berkeley a **language** is a system of signs which have in themselves neither a necessary connection, nor a similarity to the things they represent. However, for anyone who knows this system of signs, they are closely associated with the things they stand for (as signs and designata). Geometry for instance is a system of signs in booklets and books necessarily connected with its ideal counterparts. Portrait painting on the other hand would be an example of a sign system where the similarity of the painting with the person painted is of importance. It is certainly true that the painter can generally paint whatever he or she wishes. However, if he has to make a living from portrait painting, he is forced to try and make his brushwork show some similarity with the facial features of his or her model. In contrast, there is no proof of any necessary connection between something like the written or spoken language sign for the word "apple" and the well-known fruit, nor of any similarity between the forms of the word and the apple itself. Berkeley firmly believed that this was also true for the relationship between the visual ideas of sense and the ideas of the tactile sense. Every sense has its own special object or content, which to perceive it was designed: the tactile sense primarily perceives "shaped" resistance; the visual sense perceives light or its effects or component parts respectively, as colours; the sense of hearing perceives tones or the effects or mixtures of such tones as sounds or noises etc. Berkeley usually uses the expressions "ideas of sense" and "immediate objects of perception" to refer to these "objects" (colours, sounds etc.). Here, the influence of any acquired habit and the results of such a habit (i.e. more or less closely associated connections), namely all kinds of "mental additions", are to be disregarded. Thus - as we have already seen - the ideas of sense are the immediate actual and pure elements of the (sense-) experience.

Now Berkeley (in the *New Theory* et al.) claims that the visual ideas of sight are signs which, in combination, form the language that God uses to give us information about the "tactile" (material) reality. Particularly as far as survival is concerned, the tactile sense (understood as being distributed over the whole surface of the body), plays the most crucial role. It is not the dagger we see that is often deadly, but rather the one we feel.[90]

If Berkeley therefore wishes to maintain the thesis of the reality of a visual language, he has to take account of the lack of a necessary association as well as of a similarity between - briefly put - the "tactile object" and the "visual object". He is of course fully aware that this instinctively goes against the grain. Amongst other things he mentions the following two reasons for this undeniable uneasiness:

Firstly there is a certain temptation because of practical everyday language that is not suitable for purely theoretical (philosophical) purposes. For, while we speak of

---

[90] Ayers (Ed.), p. 51 f. (*New Theory of Vision,* § 147).

our ear perceiving sounds, and of our sense of smelling perceiving smells, we do not have any specific simple expressions for the immediate object of our vision and our tactile sense. We simply say that we see and feel things or objects. By saying this, we support the widely held opinion that **the object we see and the object we feel are one and the same thing**. This fosters the theoretical view of the similarity, indeed of the identity and the existence of some kind of necessary association between the object we feel and the one we see. Here we should consider, even for the sake of analogy and symmetry alone, why the visual and tactile senses of all senses should have to share a common object whilst each of our other senses can be shown to have its own immediate "sense datum".

The second reason for the above mentioned inner uneasiness lies in the conviction, which has seldom been questioned, that there are "abstract ideas", in particular the abstract idea of extension. The object's sole (abstract) extension is then thought to be the common referential object of both, the visual and the tactile senses. But such abstract ideas are (as seen) simply impossible. Therefore, neither of these two reasons, for the conviction that a common referential object for both visual and tactile senses does exist, are suitable for proving the rationality of this conviction. The suspicion might occur that this conviction is really a kind of **prejudice**, albeit really a very widely accepted one!

This is indeed Berkeley's opinion and he brings forward a row of supportive arguments. His main argument goes that objects possessing different "cartesian" dimensions cannot be identical and that they furthermore belong to **different spaces**, so to speak. The one-dimensional line cannot be lengthened by means of the ("null-dimensional") point, the area of the two-dimensional surface cannot be increased by the (one-dimensional) line. However, the immediate objects of the visual sense would be two-dimensional, those of the tactile sense three-dimensional.

Obviously, Berkeley's view of the two-dimensionality of visual ideas and the entire original field of vision needs (at first) to be explained in much more detail, then (if possible) substantiated and defended. We shall attempt to do this in the following two sections.

However, before turning at this point we should shortly discuss a further aspect of Berkeley's thesis: in the *New Theory* Berkeley obviously proceeds on the assumption that it is possible for one thing to touch another thing without an occurrence of a feeling or sensation. According to many English-speaking philosophers, this assumption concurs with knowledge derived from the "common sense". Let us take a simple example to illustrate this point: my trousers touch my legs at almost every point, but I do not feel it, at any rate not at every point and not continually. Parts of my trousers touch my shoes, but it is absolutely impossible to speak of sensations (ideas) here.

Thus, Berkeley's views in the *New* Theory et al. are a lot less eccentric than most philosophers would think it possible. This is also true for his theory (elaborated here) about the **originally** two-dimensional field of vision. Here he does not claim that the visual field of a normal adult is two-dimensional.[91] An adult's visual ideas of sense have long been so closely connected with the ideas arising from the tactile sense that the dimension of depth obviously seems to be an essential part also of the visual field. However, this is not for all people the case. Neither babies[92] nor blind people, who have regained their sight, are at once able to perceive spatially.[93]

These remarks allow us the transition to a short discussion of three ideas of the *New Theory* used by Berkeley in order to back up his main argument that has been presented briefly above. These reflections should help the reader to realize that tactile and visual ideas do not belong to the same "type or species" of ideas.

1. Assigning a new idea to one particular type or species can only take place meaningfully if this idea contains something familiar, something which has already been previously perceived. Conversely, a person who has been born blind and just gained sight, would not think that the newly acquired ideas have anything in common with previous ideas acquired through the tactile sense (cf. paragraph 128).

2. Light and colours are not only some but the **only** (immediate) objects of the visual sense; the visual form is only created through gradations of light and colour in a way similar to the technique of an impressionist painter. However, nobody would claim that these gradations can be perceived through the tactile sense (cf. paragraphs 129 and 130).

3. Furthermore, according to Berkeley, only his thesis that there is no necessary natural association between the ideas of the visual sense and those of the tactile sense can solve a number of classical optical problems. For lack of space these will only be

---

[91] Obviously, there would be a conflict between this kind of view and our own experience. However, according to Berkeley, experience is the basis and the measuring standard of truth.

[92] Cf. Developmental psychological research, e.g. the "classic" studies of Jean Piaget (and Bärbel Inhelder).
Generally speaking the research findings of Piaget and his successors substantiate the *New Theory of Vision* in many important aspects.

[93] To be more exact, colour sensations are intrinsically neither two- nor three-dimensional: however, in order to describe the probable field of vision of a formerly blind person who has recently gained sight, the use of vocabulary referring to two-dimensionality is more appropriate. The visual recognition of distance, localization and other recognition of forms of such persons can only be described as being very deficient.
Marius von Senden (*Raum- und Gestaltauffassung von operierten Blindgeborenen*, Leipzig 1932) described and analysed 66 such cases. He came to the conclusion that the patients were unable to recognize even simple shapes at first sight, although most of them claimed that they had clear tactile ideas of these shapes.

named here, but the *New Theory* contains some interesting expositions on these problems, some of which are still relevant today. The problems discussed are "Barrow's case", the problem of the "reversed retinal image", the "Molyneux Problem" and the "moon illusion".

III.2. George Berkeley's main argument for his thesis of the total disparity between the objects of the visual and the tactile senses

In 17th century geometrical optics it was generally agreed that the distance of an object to the eye, i.e. the extension of depth, is estimated by using the angle formed by the light rays that diverge from the observed object or point and the two eyes. The smaller the divergence is, the more distant the position of the object is taken to be, whereas a considerable angle indicates a near object.

Berkeley calls this conception in his *New Theory of Vision* (paragraph 19) the thesis of "natural geometry".

The aim of Berkeley's *New Theory* is to be associated with Locke's project of enlightening the human understanding about itself. The conscious elements of understanding, the ideas, are to be connected with other similar conscious elements. Berkeley holds that the (at his time) normal geometry thesis could contribute absolutely nothing here, because the question is, how the impression of the three-dimensionality of the visual field arises. And in answering this question reference to our innate capability to judge angles, which we use (if at all) unconsciously, is of no interest. Such a capability could count at the most as an optical-physiological prerequisite for the perception of depth and its philosophical explanation along the lines of Locke's project (once more: we are not ourselves conscious of any drawing of consequences from diverging angles).

Berkeley writes in paragraph 10 of his *New Theory of Vision*: "[...] no idea, which has not itself been perceived, can serve as a medium for the perception of any other idea [...]" The eye e.g. cannot perceive directly the mentally spiritual state of a person being angry but the red colour of the man who is.

One central thesis of Berkeley's is critically based on the assumption of his fellow researchers in optics that distance from the eye can be explained with a line whose end is directed from the seen object towards the eye. This produces a point on the fund of the eye, that remains unaltered despite the fact that the distance may be greater or smaller (cf. paragraph 2): but this means that distance is not represented on the retina at all (if you consider one eye or retina only). In addition to this, Berkeley develops an argument in the form of a thought experiment towards the end of his

New Theory of Vision. The experiment is about a fictional intelligent being which can see but is neither able to feel nor move.[94]

This being can not even learn the primary elements of **plane** geometry. To understand the expression "congruence" for example, it is absolutely necessary to have an idea of depth in addition to the ideas of length and width (superimposition). A being that has been completely immobile from the beginning of its existence and has not changed its position, could never comprehend the extension of depth. It could only perceive colours and light as well as their limitations and intersections. It would have no signifiers for the assumption that, if an element of light and colour increases visibly in size, anything else besides just this increase in size - namely the **approach** of the element - might be occurring. Therefore, the thesis of natural geometry proves insufficient for the following reason: it disregards completely the role played by the tactile sense (and the capability of movement which is connected with it) for a possible spatial vision.

In his (already mentioned) book *Three Dialogues between Hylas and Philonous* Berkeley differentiates between immediate and mediate or indirect sense experience. His criterion for the first kind is that only the things that have been perceived by one of the senses, are **immediately** perceived when they would have also been perceived "in the case that this sense had only just been given to us".[95] A blind person, who has just gained sight through an operation, is not able to draw the conclusion that, because the doctor's face is getting white and the nurse's red, "the doctor looks angry and the nurse looks embarrassed". We always see more than we immediately or actually see - a red stove plate appears to be hot, a clouded grain spirit bottle appears to be cold etc. According to Berkeley, depth vision belongs to this group of examples. A pale blue overcast mountain range looks very distant, whereas an unclearly contrasting hand seems to be very near the eyes. The red-hot stove plate is so closely associated with the idea of heat that it is almost impossible for us to eliminate the impression of heat when we see it. In exactly the same way the impression of great distance cannot be avoided when we see a pale blue (clue or cue 1) and partly covered (clue 2) mountain, that is additionally located in the upper field of vision (clue 3).

Berkeley is of the opinion that the construction of our field of vision is completely determined by such closely associated connections. As far as the impression of three-dimensionality is concerned, these particular clues are drawn from the area of our active tactile and movement experience. We take it for granted that a red-hot stove plate cannot look hot only, but must also feel hot.

---

[94] Cf. Ayers (Ed.), p. 53 f., (First Dialogue, §§ 153-155).
[95] Ayers (Ed.), p. 159 (First Dialogue).

Berkeley wants to convince us that visible distance (as spatial depth) is unperceivable in the same way, or better, **immediately** unperceivable.

III.3. A short discussion of Berkeley's main argument and our suggestion for a solution of the problem of visual depth perception

Wolfgang Metzger's comprehensive work *Gesetze des Sehens*[96] can be regarded as a standard work on the empirical psychology of perception. The author discusses Berkeley's theory in the eleventh chapter.

To begin with, he supports Berkeley's criticism of natural geometry to a certain extend: there is proof that we do not use what is known as "convergence" (i.e. the variable difference between the positions of the centres of the two eyes) to determine spatial depth, even though many common depth measuring instruments make use of the principle of convergence or natural geometry as their measurement basis. Thus, Metzger to a large extent accepts Berkeley's criticism of the traditional or convergence theory. By comparison, Berkeley's own positive thesis is rejected in an abrupt and undifferentiated manner. In this connection Metzger suggests that Berkeley has only one reason for his statement about spatial depth. It is the alleged insight into the fact that light rays, radiating directly from the object's point of location to the eyes, are not represented in a variable manner on the light-sensitive retina.

According to Metzger, depth dimension is represented as a width deviation of the two retinal images ("cross-disparity"): obviously this applies only to binocular and not to monocular vision. Metzger states very apodictically on page 342: "These differences in the representation of perspective are the actual basis of our binocular depth vision." Shortly afterwards, however, he adds an obviously important reservation: "We don't yet know the reason why the union of two flat **images derived from the deviations in width** to form a single visual object should produce, **of all things, differences of depth**, which are for the most part correct. All sorts of explanations have already been suggested, but none of them is really satisfactory". This means that the theory - or more appropriately - the thesis of Metzger and many others needs to be supplemented in an important respect [97]: a possible reason is, that they have chosen to ignore Berkeley's **full** thesis.

---

[96] Wolfgang Metzger, *Gesetze des Sehens*, Frankfurt/Main, 1973³.
[97] The cross-disparity theory has nevertheless been included in numerous encyclopaedia and school text-books as a "scientifically" proven explanation of depth vision.

It was probably unavoidable that the alternative theories built on the concepts "binocularity" and "cross-disparity" have also been criticized. One of these critics is Alfred Politz with his essay *On the Origin of Space Perception*.[98] Here he first refers to the fact that the transfer from one dimension to another (from the second to the third) is, literally speaking, a "drastic" one. We have to imagine, as far as this is actually possible, living in a two-dimensional world, and to consider how radically such a world would differ from ours.

Politz holds it to be true that there are differences in the two retinal images in which the depth dimension is functionally represented. However, there would still be two-dimensional **images** present which represent three-dimensional objects. The so-to-speak qualitative leap (Hegel) into the perceivable third dimension would still be very problematic, even if we take the disparity of the retinal images into account.

Furthermore, some well-known observations we make in our everyday life could lead us to have reasonable doubt that binocularity of all things should be the actual source of three-dimensional vision. The majority of living beings e.g. have eyes on the sides of their heads, which would suggest that they have very inadequate spatial perception or none at all. In fact, we do not get this impression. Consider, for instance, how accurately a predatory fish locates and attacks its prey with regard to distance of depth. According to Politz, people who only have one eye, are able to judge distances very accurately (are not some good Badminton players?).

He deduces from this that the impression of three-dimensionality is not necessarily connected with binocularity. Politz claims that a new-born child develops this impression gradually as it tries to reach and catch things, turns around and so on. This would mean that firstly an elementary concept of spatiality has to be created through touch and kinaesthesia before the visual sense can make use of the specific perceptual clues which indicate depth: also in our opinion this is an interesting statement, especially when applied to Berkeley's comprehensive understanding of the origins of visual depth. This implies further that in principle a person, who has only one (functioning) eye, develops his three-dimensional field of vision in precisely the same way as a person with two eyes.

A conclusion can gradually be drawn here. As we think, **both theses**, the new "natural geometry" thesis (Metzger et al.) and the (neo-) Berkeleyian thesis (Politz et al.), are both correct in one aspect and wrong in another. In explaining this statement we would first like to clarify the meaning of the expression **"3-D effect"**. This is important as the concept will play a crucial role in our (simple) solution of the visual depth problem. The 3-D effect is the specific impression of binocular seeing that we **ourselves** are bodily actually present in the space belonging to our own field of

---

[98] Alfred Politz, "On the Origin of Space Perception", in: *Philosophy and Phenomenological Research* 40 (1979/80), pp. 258-264.

vision. The easiest method of testing for this is to close one eye (and even better: the other partly) and then open it again. Vision using one eye seems very detached, as if we were looking through a hole in a wall, or, through our orbital cavity. It is interesting to note that the impression, that the field of vision expands in depth, does **not** disappear any more than the basic ability to judge distances does. What we do loose, when we look through one eye, is simply a certain "feeling" (which is more easily experienced than explained). This is precisely the feeling which should be defined as the *3-D effect*.

Now, the cross-disparity of the retinal images appears to be in causal relationship with this 3-D effect. We can find a good argument for this supposition if we consider the way a stereoscope works. A stereoscope is a device that allows us to perceive two slightly differing two-dimensional images three-dimensionally. The two different images of an object produce the effect that we feel to be present with that object in **one and the same** space. The 3-D effect occurs when an image has been photographed (or filmed) from two slightly different positions - corresponding to the points of the two eyes - and these slightly differing images are also represented on the left and the right eye-ground.

We would like now to suggest the following difference which is simple enough and, as far as we know, original:

On the one hand we have the 3-D effect and **on the other hand** we have the three-dimensional field of vision which includes the extension of depth. The latter is not necessarily associated with the 3-D effect, as we just learnt by looking through one eye only. We suspect, (only) partly following Metzger's lines, that the 3-D effect casually depends upon the cross-disparity of the retinal images, although this is perhaps not the only cause. Conversely we presume - as Berkeley would have done - that the three-dimensionally extended vision of depth is caused by very closly associated connections of certain visual "clues" and tactile-kinetic experiences. Such clues, independent of the specific 3-D effect, seem to be quite sufficient, especially for judging distances.

(To repeat:) The essence of the problem of visual depth is:

Does its origin lie in binocularity or in the associative overlapping of tactile and visual experiences? A straightforward suggestion for solving this problem is to differentiate between three-dimensional vision and the 3-D effect. We would like to relate the latter to binocularity and cross-disparity, whereas the former is in our view rather the result of projection and association as described by Berkeley and his followers. In conclusion it should be pointed out that we consider this suggestion of a *simple solution* to consist of two theses, which both can as such be tested (according to Popper's scientific criterion of "potential falsification"; although we personally do consider this test far too restrictive). Obviously it is relatively easy to test the relationship between binocularity and the 3-D effect under the principle of potential falsification. You close one eye (even better: and the second partly) and try to find out whether your visual impression retains the 3-D effect.

The following exemplary test is **one** ("down-to-earth") possibility of applying the falsification principle to the relationship between three-dimensional vision and the results of gradually developing association (or projection of tactile ideas into visual ones): a newly-born living creature, for example a calf, is blindfolded and we wait and observe whether or not this animal can find the udder, or the mother's milk respectively. If this is **not** the case, the thesis mentioned above would probably have to be dropped for the following reason: if the blindfolded calf does not find the udder, it is clear that new-born calves use their eyes primarily for orientation, without having to wait for associations with ideas of touch. Once more: this result would conflict with the consequence of Berkeley's doctrine that has approvingly been used for explaining the three-dimensional field of vision. Accordingly a certain amount of time has to pass before the capability of perceiving three-dimensionally is developed. This development, or "maturing process", is the result of the close association of visual clues and tactile-kinetic experiences. On the basis of Berkeley's thesis we would therefore expect that a new-born calf does not use the visual sense but rather the sense of smell or touch for orientation purposes when searching for the udder (in other words, the calf could orientate itself successfully even when blindfolded).

But if the opposite result did occur (that is, what we would expect), then Berkeley's main argument would be clearly, if not conclusively, confirmed. Accordingly, the field of vision would appear to be (somewhat similar to) two-dimensional originally and therefore the constituent objects of this field, which are visually perceived (the ideas), would have to be regarded as being entirely (?) different from the tactile objects (the material things). Any natural science or language-analytical explanation of their necessary mutual relationships (which are so important for our life and survival), must then certainly appear at least controversial.

III.4. Concluding notes

In contrast to many other philosopher-theologians of his day, Berkeley was not content with an (his) argument for the *existence* of God (the subject of our first and - in parts - second chapter). An additional aim was also to show the plausibility of the belief in **divine providence**. He fulfils this aim by demonstrating that the ideas of vision, namely light and colours in their manifold combinations, can be regarded as a kind of visual language by which God speaks to his creatures. He, namely the cosmic spirit Berkeley had previously discussed and "demonstrated", uses this language to continually provide us with important information about corporeal reality.

To achieve this goal, Berkeley firstly has to show that there are no logically necessary or naturally explainable relationships between the ideas of vision and the ideas of touch. Secondly he has to show that the lack of such relationships is the distinguishing mark for language, which is paradigmatically considered artificial and conventional. His main argument is that the different sorts of ideas just mentioned belong to differing dimensions. Furthermore (and in consequence of this), they are related to different objects, i.e. ideas and things. Beginning with the important objection raised by modern psychologists concerning the problem of visual depth, we have tried to offer a simple solution roughly along Berkeley's lines: binocularity is only responsible for the "3-D effect" and the ideas of touch and motion - so we thought - are still (i.e. also after Metzger et al.) indispensable for the development of the third dimension in the visual field.

One final point should perhaps be mentioned here already: with regard to Berkeley's argument for a divine providence in the *New Theory* (as in the *Theory ... Vindicated and Explained* and *Alciphron*) the question must arise whether this argument fits into the immaterialistic framework. As we have seen, the existence of material things is not allowed inside this framework and it is therefore denied too that ideas (of touch) can be the causal effects of these things in themselves. But, if these immaterialistic theses are maintained, do they not destroy the basis of Berkeley's argument for a divine providence? Fortunately for him this need not to be the case. Berkeley's arguments rest on the disparity of ideas of touch and ideas of vision and the proposition that there are no natural connections between them: and this holds or stays true also within Berkeley's immaterialistic context where it is the will and acting of God that delivers different series of ideas (one for each sense) into our consciousness. But this means (against the first impression) that it makes no essential difference for the "providence argument" whether the ideas of touch originate in matter or in (God's) mind. Essential for this argument is only that no natural (scientific) explanation for the orderly occurrence of the intrinsically different series of ideas of sense is possible - or that the *permanent miracle* comes into the reader's view.

IV. The Argument for God's Activity in Nature (*De motu*)

IV.0 Preliminary remarks

Berkeley wanted to verify the concept of divine providence by means of the disparity between the ideas of the senses of touch and vision. These different aspects of perception are not linked by nature but rather by (divine) "art". Thus, the visible world exists only within the conscious mind, whereas the tactile world also exists beyond it - at least according to the *New Theory of Vision*. This claim is retracted in Berkeley's later work, the *Principles*: **everything** that is perceived is connected with God's mind, tactile sensations as well as visual ones; to stake a different claim would be a "vulgar error", and only a special treatise on vision would hardly have been a suitable place to clear up such an error.[99] If we accept this to be true, does then the evidence of divine providence collapse after its basis has been removed like this? The answer has to be: in its original form, yes. However (as we have just seen), only a little effort is necessary for modifying this form. The disparity between tactile and visual impressions remains as an experienced fact; thus, for example, we perceive no similarity between the tactile sensation of the smoothness of an apple and the visual sensation of its redness. What becomes irrelevant, is the relatively unsubstantial claim, or at least the suggestion in the *New Theory*, that this disparity is connected with the different forms of existence of the tactile world (as elements of the "exterior" world) and the visual world (as elements of the "interior" world).

In this respect a language different from that of the *New Theory* (and the *Theory ... Vindicated and Explained* as well as *Alciphron*) is used in the *Principles*. Man cannot escape the sphere of consciousness, as he is not able to reach (with his mind) a world which allegedly exists beyond mind. For, if we take a closer look at this world of the things in themselves, it is neither perceptible nor even conceivable. However, man can escape from the sphere of **his** own consciousness, entering into the "infinite sphere" of the divine consciousness - and he **is already there** with the perception of every idea, which he himself has found in his mind (but not in dreams), i.e. through the perception of an "idea of sense". The object observed here is neither the observer himself nor a part of him. We have to look for the underlying reason for the joint occurrences of the perceptions of the smoothness and redness of the apple outside our perception, but not in the completely imperceptible superfluous unthinking ("stupid"[100]) and indeed unthinkable (material) substance. This is even clearer in the case of our remarkable capacity of transcending the sphere of our own consciousness, where

---

[99] Cf. Ayers (Ed.), p. 89 (*Principles*, § 44).
[100] Cf. Ayers (Ed.), p. 106 (*Principles*, § 93).

we perceive ideas, that we have not produced ourselves and whose existence is not related conditionally at all to our own minds (with the execption of their unity). Through the strength of God's power, and not through our own power or that of the matter itself, we are pushed beyond our own subjectivity into the realm of the ideas of sense. It belongs to the provident grace of God that allows us to "enjoy" objectivity, reality (and together with these, divinity, so to speak).

The Irish bishop attempts to further substantiate this idea of divine providence, or the idea of the grace of God, in and within the natural perceivable world. He clearly considered the argument of the preceeding chapter to contain still too much speculation and not enough conclusive "proof", thought it possibly to "be wobbly on its legs" so to speak. A fundamental proof of **divine activity** in the corporeal world or **in nature** is searched for and offered in order to give further support to his concept of providence. Such a concept requires, as will be made clear, a rather modern "instrumentalist" (non-realist) interpretation of (natural) science.

IV.1. Berkeley's "instrumentalist" tendencies in his philosophy of language

Berkeley's conception of science is deeply influenced by his idea of the function of language: the sign system known as language was primarily created by humans in order to facilitate both survival and life, i.e. its function was pragmatic not theoretical. During the early development of the sciences of mathematics, physics, chemistry etc. (the non-metaphysical sciences) expectations may have been different - or they may always have been the same - this does not alter the fact that (for Berkeley) these sign systems are also primarily pragmatic and of limited theoretical value only.

The best way of approaching Berkeley's theory of science is to take a look at his philosophy of language and its "instrumentalist" tendencies. By doing this, a further contribution to shedding some light upon his criticism of the "abstract general idea of material substance" can perhaps be made.

- Berkeley also starts out in his philosophy of language as a (critical) follower of John Locke. This "precursor" pointed out at the beginning of the third book of his famous *Essay*, that the function of words is to represent ideas in the mind, whereby the per se subjective can be intersubjectively communicated. Words are signs that are perceived through the senses ear, eye, and sometimes touch and which represent ideas that can always only be sensually perceived by one person. Looking at it this way, the idea is the meaning of the word and it is easy to reach the conclusion that a word, which is not based on an idea, has no meaning. Berkeley's intention of "no word to be used without an idea"[101] in the early *Philosophical Commentaries* is exactly in keeping with this thought. However, it is worth mentioning that he already showed doubts about the practicability of his maxim only a few pages later: "Qu: How can all words be said to stand for ideas?"[102] In his extensive book *Alciphron*, a critical seven-dialogue work about the "free-thinkers" (published a quarter of a century later in 1732), he even puts his original ideas of the philosophy of language into the mouth of his imaginary major **antagonist**, Alciphron ("the minute philosopher": a fictional character, but very reminiscent of Lord Shaftsbury): "words are signs: they do or should stand for ideas, which so far as they suggest they are significant. But words that suggest no ideas are insignificant."[103] What Alciphron is driving at here is that people who are sensible and think critically cannot (out of linguistic reasons) seriously accept the Christian religion. Certain expressions such as "grace" and "trinity" play a very important role in this doctrine and are yet in Alciphron's view meaningless words. This, because we really have no (clear) idea of what "grace" actually is: "What is the clear and distinct idea marked by the word grace?"[104]

How does Euphranor (Berkeley) reply to this attack? Firstly a clear and definite idea as meaning has not to be found, as only a few words are proper names and as such connected with clear ideas whereas most words are in contrast general expressions (related only to "concepts"). However, it is not the case that these general words are connected with clear (abstract) ideas, as examples such as **man, the** triangle, **the** colour and many others show. Our language sets pitfalls for our thinking here. Instead of saying "all men are mortal", we can also express ourselves in the following way: "man is mortal". In the first case we think vaguely of an enormous number of different people - our idea is a general one. In the second case we want to think vaguely of a universal man and imagine that we have a general abstract idea. The "idea" is not clear or definite in either of the two cases; in the latter it can even be definitively excluded that any idea at all exists. We cannot form an idea of something which is totally impossible. (This man would have to be young and old, man and woman etc.) It is of no decisive importance whether the idea is understood as being a thing produced by our

---

[101] Ayers (Ed.), p. 290 (*Philosophical Commentaries*, Notebook A, No. 422).
[102] Ayers (Ed.), p. 298 (*Philosophical Commentaries*, Notebook A, No. 494). Berkeley later explicitly denies that every concept has to correspond to an idea. Cf. e.g. Ayers (Ed.), p. 104 (*Principles*, § 89).
[103] *Alciphron*, Seventh Dialogue, Sect. 2 (in: *The Works of George Berkeley, Bishop of Cloyne*, Volume III, ed. by A.A. Luce and T.E. Jessop, p. 287).
[104] Ibid., p. 290 (Seventh Dialogue, § 4).

power of imagination or as the object of our "intellect". The fact remains that every idea is something individual or an individual something and can therefore not contain any contradictory elements within itself (also: above and below 1.70 m of height, more or less than 70 kilos in weight, etc.). According to Berkeley's nominalistic thesis, **man** as such does not exist, either *in re* or *in intellectu*. "Man is mortal" therefore is not a statement about the nature or essence of mankind, but merely a reasonable stylistic transformation of the sentence: "all men are mortal". We have to return to the latter and accept that the expression "men" may become meaningful, either through the vague idea of many people or (as this would never extend to all people), through an idea (the difficulties of this conception have already been mentioned) of a particular person who is thought of as representing all mankind.

Evidently, the **behaviour** of the listener is aimed at in the first place, when someone speaks of "grace" in a sermon for example. Theological tracts that deal with the concept of grace have to be based at least on a vague idea (which is usually indeed to be found). Similar vague but stimulating ideas can be encountered often enough also in text-books for physics where the concept of "force" is discussed. As soon as I go beyond merely reciting a formula (like: F = ma) and try really to imagine what force is, or rather more exactly imagine force or power itself - disregarding the object which is producing it - I will run into great difficulties. But nevertheless, the pure concept of force has certainly contributed to the advancement of physical science as well as to the art of engineering; therefore this concept of power is certainly **useful**. However, "ought we not therefore, by a parity of reason, to conclude there may be possibly divers true and useful propositions concerning the one as well as the other [physics as well as theology]?"[105] The pragmatic-instrumental idea can already be found stated in such sentences. The "Introduction" to the *Principles* shows even more clearly that this non-theoretical function of language (for Berkeley) does not lie somewhere on the periphery of this system of signs, but rather vice versa. Language originates first and foremost from the contexts of life and activity and therefore (Locke's) "communicating of ideas" is **not** the chief end of language:

> Besides, the communicating of ideas marked by words is not the chief and only end of language, as is commonly supposed. There are other ends, as the raising of some passion, the exciting to, or deterring from an action, the putting the mind in some particular disposition; to which

---

[105] ibid., p. 296 (Seventh Dialogue, § 7).

the former is in many cases barely subservient, and sometimes entirely omitted [...] [106]

That language has repeatedly misled philosophers can be attributed to the fact that it came into existence for other than theoretical purposes - Berkeley is never weary of repeating this claim. It is true that Berkeley never expects his philosophy to provide an "entire deliverance from the deception of words"[107], though he does promise us a deliverance that is at least partial. A good example for this is paragraph 49 of the *Principles* where he points out the way in which we are tempted to believe in material substance because of the superficial similarity of the structures of language and the world. In the sentence "a die is hard, extended and square" the grammatical subject, the die, is given predicates. This leads us to believe that the object in the world must be correspondingly structured and that a (material) substance must be equipped with differing qualities from which the independence or substantiality of the material "carrier" ("substratum") seems to follow somehow.

This I cannot comprehend: to me a die seems to be nothing distinct from those things which are termed its modes or accidents. And to say a die is hard, extended and square, is not to attribute those qualities to a subject distinct from and supporting them, but only an explication of the meaning of the word *die*. [108]

IV.2. Force (Power) and motion: *De motu*

We perceive motion in nature mainly through our sense of vision, but also by means of touch and hearing. It is totally impossible to doubt this.[109] However, some doubt still remains (amongst other things) about the question whether the causes of motion, known as "forces" or "powers", can also be perceived. Locke's answer to this question does not seem very convincing or definite. He writes that the mind infers the presence of power somewhere from certain sensual impressions. In the next sentence we find, however:

---

[106] Ayers (Ed.), p. 74 (*Principles*, "Introduction", § 20).
[107] Ibid., p. 75 (*Principles*, § 23).
[108] Ayers (Ed.), p. 91, (*Principles*, § 49).
[109] The Eleatics also never questioned the *perception* of motion. Neither did Descartes, who claims that God creates the world anew every moment in a *creatio continua* (thus creating the mere "appearance" of motion).

> But yet, if we will consider it attentively, bodies, by our senses, do not afford us so clear and distinct an idea of active power as we have from reflection on the operations of our minds. [110]

Afterwards Berkeley claimed that originally we acquire the concept of power by reflecting on ourselves, but then we carry out a suspicious projective transfer, and later believe that we perceive power where we see moving bodies that are more or less similar to ourselves: first our fellow-men, then also animals, growing plants, rolling stones etc. Of course, Berkeley continues to say, we are not identical with our bodies but **spirits**, and therefore attributing power to spiritless things is already empirically unjustified. No body moves itself - a "universal [spiritual] agent" is at work throughout nature: **God**.

This is a first rough outline of Berkeley's doctrine of motion and power. We shall now give a more comprehensive account of his ideas, using details taken mainly from his work *De motu*.[111] It was written in 1720 during Berkeley's visit to France where he had heard that the Paris Royal Academy of Science was offering a prize for a treatise on the theory of motion. Berkeley handed in his treatise but was not awarded a prize. However, he had it printed and it was finally published in London in 1721. The treatise comprises 72 paragraphs or sections with an average length of about half a printed page. It starts getting interesting in the fourth paragraph:

> We perceive [...] in heavy bodies falling an accelerated motion towards the centre of the earth; and that is all the senses tell us. By reason, however, we infer that there is some cause or principle of these phenomena, and that is popularly called *gravity*. But since the cause of the fall of heavy bodies is unseen and unknown, gravity in that usage cannot properly be styled a sensible quality. It is, therefore, an occult quality. But what an occult quality is, or how any quality can act or do anything, we can scarcely conceive - indeed we cannot conceive. And so men would do better to let the occult quality go, and attend only to the sensible effects. [112]

When we think about the falling motion of objects, we imagine the force of gravity which (in principle) has to be defined as an imperceptible, i.e. "occult", property of nature. However, as long as the statement counts that "what is itself occult explains nothing"[113], we would be wiser to stick to things that are

---
[110] Cf. *Essay*, Second Book, Ch. 21, Sect. 4.
[111] In: Ayers (Ed.), pp. 211-227, (in an Engl. translation by A.A .Luce - *Of Motion*).
[112] In: Ayers (Ed.), p. 211 (*Principles*, § 4).
[113] Ibid., p. 212 (*Principles*, § 6).

perceptible. As in the case of gravity, similar rules apply for powers in general. But the concepts of power and gravity are therefore not completely superfluous. They could play a role in the theory of motion similar to the use of universal terms in language which are sometimes used to abbreviate and generalize propositions. This pragmatic advantage should not lead us to make conclusions about the reality of the things though, i.e. that general objects, "universals", do really exist. To make language more efficient and to speak about the nature of things, are two completely different matters. Some things may serve the purposes of mechanics (physics in general): "But to be of service to reckoning and mathematical demonstrations is one thing, to set forth the nature of things is another."[114]

Similarly, Hylas already made the remark in the *Dialogues*:

> [...] but you know ordinary practice does not require a nicety of speculative knowledge. Hence the vulgar retain their mistakes, and for all that, make a shift to bustle through the affairs of life. But philosophers know better things.[115]

As proof of these statements Berkeley could point to the fact that we usually speak about sunrise, sunset and the orbiting of the sun, whereas it is actually the earth that moves. However, he may also have been thinking of his own immaterialistic doctrine which sometimes forces him to seek refuge in the following maxim: "in such things we ought to *think with the learned, and speak with the vulgar.*"[116]

In his opinion the representatives of modern mechanical physics also follow (unwittingly) this maxim. Modern physics, in contrast to the physics of antiquity and the post-classical Aristotelian tradition, no longer recognized any major difference between a mechanically produced "artificial product" and a "natural object". Regularities which are found in "artificial experiments" can thus be transferred to natural objects and situations. Berkeley principally thought highly of this kind of "pure" physics. Unlike Galilei, Descartes considered animate objects to be suitably and adequately explained by mechanical physics, too. Leibniz almost took the opposite direction here by transferring the concept of "alive power" ("lebendige Kraft") as shown in animate objects also to inanimate objects and replacing the *extensio* as the essential criterion of an object by *vis*.[117] Berkeley does not disagree with the use of the expression "forces" or "powers" in

---

[114] Ibid., p. 214 (*Principles*, § 18).
[115] In: Ayers (Ed.), p. 181 (Third Dialogue, near the beginning).
[116] Ayers (Ed.), p. 92 (*Principles*, § 51).
[117] Cf. G.W. Leibniz, *Specimen dynamicum*, Acta Eruditorum 1695 (var. editions).

physics, although he considers them to be merely metaphorical and thereby denies that a natural phenomenon thereby can really be explained. However, when he is thinking and speaking for himself, he keeps to the "learned", to be more exact, (at least in *De motu*) to the scholarly Cartesians.

> Let us see then what sense and experience tell us, and reason that rests upon them. There are two supreme classes of things, body and soul. By the help of sense we know the extended thing, solid, mobile, figured and endowed with other qualities which meet the senses, but the sentient, percipient, thinking thing we know by a certain internal consciousness [...] All that which we know to which we have given the name *body* contains nothing in itself which could be the principle of motion or its efficient cause; for impenetrability, extension and figure [the characteristics of body] neither include nor connote any power of producing motion [...] [118]

Every man finds without possible doubts **within himself or herself** the power to act. When scholars like Leibniz claim that powers are also to be found in inanimate objects, they refer to an unknown "power" which is an occult property, and thus they unwillingly confess to their own ignorance:

> The contents of the idea of body we know; but what we know in body is agreed not to be the principle of motion. But those who as well maintain something unknown in body of which they have no idea and which they call the principle of motion, are in fact simply stating that the principle of motion is unknown, and one would be ashamed to linger long on subtleties of this sort. [119]

Referring to occult properties does not contribute at all to the explanation of natural phenomena, it rather stands in the way of a **true** explanation. Motion as an undeniable fact of nature is like the two-faced head of Janus: one side faces the senses - we perceive its effect - the other remains hidden in the dark; we have no experience of its cause or causes. Light only falls on one place in the darkness and this place is in ourselves. "Personal experience" teaches us: "Our mind at will can stir and stay the movements of our limbs." [120] This is where we can succeed by ourselves in experiencing the cause of movement and the spiritual quality of motion in general. Why should we not be allowed to accept a spiritual principle as the origin of movements in nature then? For this reason it is not necessary to

---
[118] Ayers (Ed.), p. 215 (*De motu*, § 21 f.).
[119] Ayers (Ed.), p. 215 (*De motu*, § 24).
[120] Ayers (Ed.), p. 216 (*De motu*, § 25).

deny the fact that there are "powers" at work in nature, but we cannot limit our explanation to this statement alone. Similarly there is nothing to prevent us from saying that there are "powers" at work within ourselves, except for the fact that we may have a certain feeling that such a statement is no longer very enlightening.

Berkeley is well aware of the fact that his ideas concerning the possibility of a spiritual principle or the spirit of God being active in nature are in no way original. However, he does not intend to make such a claim and so he even explicitly refers to the long philosophical history of this idea himself:

> Anaxagoras was the first to introduce *nous* to impress motion on inert matter. Aristotle, too, approves that opinion and confirms it in many ways, openly stating that the first mover is immovable, indivisible, and has no magnitude. And he rightly notes that to say that every mover must be moveable is the same as to say that every builder must be capable of being built. *Phys.* Bk. 8. Plato, moreover, in the Timaeus records that this corporeal machine, or visible world, is moved and animated by mind which eludes all sense. Today indeed Cartesian philosophers recognize God as the principle of natural motions. And Newton everywhere frankly intimates that not only did motion originate from God, but that still the mundane system is moved by the same acts. This is agreeable to Holy Scripture; this is approved by the opinion of the Schoolmen [...] [121]

IV.3. Berkeley as a precursor of Duhem

If mechanics and physics are not really competent for the true explanations of movements and changes in nature, where does the field of interest of these sciences lie then? The answer can only be: in the account of only so-called causes, the "occasional" causes which are in reality nothing but signs for the fuller organization and future sequencing of the collections of ideas of sense. Thus smoke, for example, is the only so-called effect of the occasional or secondary "cause" fire. Somehow the will of an enormous cosmic spirit seems to be acting as the effective or primary ("real") cause of change beneath the surface of natural occurrences. Thus, the researcher's knowledge of nature does not differ from that of a layman in that he would have a more profound knowledge of the real causes. However, he does have a more comprehensive view of the relationship between natural events which allows him (guided by his knowledge

---

[121] Ayers (Ed.), p. 217 (*Principles*, § 32). When referring to the Cartesian philosophers, Berkeley is certainly thinking primarily of Malebranche.

of the laws in nature) to make assumptions about past and (in the first place) predictions about future events. Paragraph 105 of the *Principles* provides us with a concise summary of Berkeley's philosophy of science:

> If therefore we consider the difference there is betwixt natural philosophers and other men, with regard to their knowledge of the *phenomena*, we shall find it consists, not in an exacter knowledge of the efficient cause that produces them, for that can be no other than the *will of a spirit*, but only in a greater largeness of comprehension, whereby analogies, harmonies, and agreements are discovered in the works of Nature, and the particular effects explained, that is, reduced to general rules [...], which rules grounded on the analogy, and uniformness observed in the production of natural effects, are most agreeable, and sought after by the mind; for that they extend our prospect beyond what is present, and near to us, and enable us to make very probable conjectures, touching things that may have happened at very great distances of time and place, as well as to predict things to come; which sort of endeavour towards omniscience, is much affected by the mind. [122]

Thus the aim of natural science is to achieve a more comprehensive overall understanding of natural phenomena by ordering them firstly **according to general rules (laws of nature) in a functional manner**, secondly in **"natural histories"** based on the same rules, and finally in ("instruments" of) **forecasts of future natural occurrences**. The last function mentioned can be regarded as the major aim of natural science, whereas the two earlier functions are necessary preconditions for its fulfillment. Thus modern science, and particularly modern (mathematical) physics, can be regarded as an **instrument of prediction**. Science is not so much a thoroughgoing explanation of past or present natural occurrences, but far more a pragmatic aid for prediction.

Paragraph 58 of the *Principles* contains an example of such an *instrumentalist* interpretation of (astro-)physics. Berkeley alludes here to the famous disagreement between Galileo Galilei and Cardinal Bellarmin and comments:

> [...] the question, whether the earth moves or no, amounts in reality to no more than this, to wit, whether we have reason to conclude from what hath been observed by astronomers, that if we were placed in such and such circumstances, and such or such a position and distance, both from the earth and sun, we should perceive the former to move

---
[122] Ayers (Ed.), p. 109 (*Principles*, § 105).

among the choir of planets, and appearing in all respects like one of them: and this, by the established rules of Nature, which we have no reason to mistrust, is reasonably collected from the phenomena. [123]

Berkeley's theory of the philosophy of science experienced a remarkable and unexpected renaissance at the turn of the last century - ironically as if these theses were something entirely new though. At least at the beginning of the development of their ideas, Ernst Mach, Karl Pearson, Henri Poincaré and Pierre Duhem seem hardly to have taken any notice of Berkeley's work at all. This makes it even more amazing that they have such a lot of ideas in common with our eighteenth century Irish bishop. In the case of Mach for example this has been shown by Karl Popper.[124] However, Mach's underlying philosophical assumptions are completely opposite to Berkeley's; in other words, they only have the theoretical surface in common.

In the case of Duhem however we find the real continuation of Berkeley's philosophy of science. Both show a deep respect for two (possible) forms of knowledge, common sense (sens commun, bon sens) and metaphysics (Mach by the way scorned both forms). The "bon sens" and the everyday believes associated with it about "how things are" (that is to say more or less "what they look like"), are not only, according to Duhem, not disproved by physics - what is even more, physics on the contrary does have to rely on the common sense of the physicist. As the science of physics does not study the true nature of objects, it cannot clash with the ordinary world's view of objects. In *La théorie physique, son objet et sa structure*[125] the French scientist and historian writes as follows: "thus, physical theory never gives us the explanation of experimental laws; it never reveals realities hiding under the sensible appearance."[126] For Duhem "explanation" ("expliquer") has to be intuitively understood like this: "to strip reality of the appearances covering it like a veil."[127]

It is absolutely essential for Duhem that the researcher uses his common sense. This is primarily understood as the kind of sound judgement which is

---

[123] Ibid., p. 94. Cf. also Ayers (Ed.), p. 218 (*De motu*, § 35): "It is not [...] in fact the business of physics to establish efficient causes, but only the rules of impulsions or attractions."

[124] Cf. K. Popper, "A Note on Berkeley as a Precursor of Mach", in: *The British Journal for the Philosophy of Science* 4, (1954), pp. 26-36.

[125] Original edition: Pierre Duhem, *La théorie physique, son objet et sa structure*, Paris 1906.

[126] P. Duhem, *The Aim and Structure of Physical Theory*, transl. P. P. Wiener, New York 1962., p. 26. Berkeley writes in *De motu* § 18: "To be of service to reckoning and mathematical demonstrations is one thing, to set forth the nature of things is another."; in: Ayers (Ed.), p. 219.

[127] Duhem., p. 7, (Ch. 1).

necessary when a problem cannot be solved by clear logical deduction from certain premises or by using accepted theories. It is absolutely essential in the process of selecting hypotheses, and - in connection with this - particularly important in the decision-making processes involved in these phases of scientific development, that later came to be known as "critical" and even "revolutionary" (Th. Kuhn). Duhem mentions as an example the ("pre-Einstein") age, in which the foundations of Newton's theory of the corpuscular emission theory of light were rocked by various new experiments. Furthermore, he makes the following comments about Biot, who after being initially reluctant to do so, completely changed his mind and joined the reformers, the wave or undulation theorists:

> After Foucault's experiment had shown that light travelled faster in air than in water, Biot gave up supporting the emission hypothesis; strictly, pure logic would not have compelled him to give it up, for Foucault's experiment was not the crucial experiment that Arago thought he saw in it, but by resisting wave optics for a longer time Biot would have been lacking in good sense. [128]

Moreover, in other writings about the undulation theory he claims that it is illusory to believe that the real reason for those properties, which we perceive as colour and light, lies in "oscillation": If we think of the to-and-fro motions of a real body ("air" or "aether"), then we are mistaken: "we are [in this physical hypothesis] only imagining an abstract quantity, a purely mathematical expression [...] This oscillation is to our mind a representation, not an explanation".[129] **This image is not veridical,** but useful. It can help us to set our intuitions at work. Once again the science of physics cannot exist without "that confused collection of tendencies, aspirations, and intuitions" which are indissolubly associated with common sense.[130] Duhem does not think much of the familiar value-free research as it is described and advocated so strongly in the writings of Max Weber. On the contrary, the successful testing of a hypothesis is always combined with moral behaviour:

> We are thus led to the conclusion so clearly expressed by Claude Bernard: the sound experimental criticism of a hypothesis is subordinated to certain moral conditions; in order to estimate correctly the agreement of a physical theory with the facts, it is not enough to be

---

[128] Ibid., p. 218, (Ch. 10).
[129] Ibid., p. 30, (Ch. 2).
[130] Cf. ibid., p. 104, (Ch. 4).

a good mathematician and skilful experimenter; one need also be an impartial and faithful judge. [131]

As we can see from this quotation, Duhem (as indeed in many other things) bases his methodology on that of Blaise Pascal. The experimental results in an area of research (e.g. electromagnetic radiation) are to be put together in a hypothetical theory and by reflecting on this theory conclusions are to be drawn deductively, and can then be tested empirically; therefore appropriate experiments have to be thought up and carried out. If the results of these are in agreement with the predictions, then the degree of certainty of the theory has risen. The theory may then even be called "true" (at least for the time being). These words, "truth" and "certainty", do not have the deeper metaphysical correspondence-theoretical meaning ("correspondence with the things behind the veil of the images or models"): they only express the "correspondence" of the conclusions of the theory with the laws and hypotheses on which the theory has been grounded.[132] Nevertheless, understanding the theory in this manner does allow some objectivity. It can be the "proven" element of a general and unifying background theory. We can believe reasonably but not dogmatically that, in accounting for the experienced facts, this background theory has a logical order that somehow reflects an ontological one, although we cannot strictly prove this.[133]

Such ideas go far beyond those found in Berkeley's writings, but they continue along the same lines of thinking. Both emphasize the short-comings of physical theories and criticize the scientific practice that, where an explanation would be required (e.g. for what actually causes bodies to be attracted to each other), sometimes only a word (such as "gravitation") or a formula is provided.[134] They both regard the supplication of an overview concerning the phenomena of nature as the primary task of the science of physics. Thus we read in the works of Duhem:

> A physical theory is not an explanation. It is a system of mathematical propositions, deduced from a small number of principles which aim to

---

[131] Ibid., p. 218, (Ch. 10).
[132] Cf. ibid., Part II, (Ch. 4). For Pascal see: Manfred Heeß, *Blaise Pascal - Wissenschaftliches Denken und christlicher Glaube*, München 1979.
[133] Cf. ibid., Part I, (Ch. II, § 4). This is an important remainder of Duhem's theory of science.
[134] Cf. Berkeley, *Principles*, § 103 ff.; Duhem, *Aim and Structure*, Ch. 3.

represent as simply, as completely, and as exactly as possible a set of experimental laws. [135]

Furthermore, both refer to the instrumental-prognostic character of physics (physics as an instrument of prognostics) and the necessity of supplementing this usage with metaphysics. They even agree here down to such detail as that the "necessity to expand" should not be confused with "blending".[136] Both confirm several times that they hold *common sense* in high esteem and can also be shown to have even more details in common.[137]

IV.4. The idea of a visible God

The epistemological "position" of Descartes, Locke and all other "scientific realists" seems to suffer in this dilemma: either they begin with the "representations", never arriving at the objects represented at all as they cannot compare them with their representations. Or, on the other hand, they begin with the "external objects", and it is not made clear how these can become conscious representations or "ideas". The problem becomes even more conspicuous when we consider the relation supposed (according to this theory) to exist between the external objects and their mental representations on closer examination. We will find then that this is an attempt at thinking of things that are not easy to combine in only one relationship. The problem is that this relationship is at the same time thought to be a physical and an epistemological one. Furthermore, the causal relationship cannot simply assume the role of the cognitive one and it is difficult to imagine the reverse process. Also, we cannot regard the physical and the epistemological relation as being two different relations, thus losing the scientific character of the "causal" theory of representation. The acceptance of a relation between the epistemological subject and its object separated from its - in the widest sense of the word "physical" (and also chemical and bio-physiological) - basis, is nothing short of the completely unscientific postulate of an "intuition" or intellectual "Anschauung". Therefore, a relationship in scientific realism, considered from the differing ends, has to take on two roles or perform two tasks

---

[135] Ibid., p. 13, (Ch. 2).

[136] Duhem seems to have been a supporter of the Aristotelian metaphysics (cf. the introduction to the German transl. *Ziel und Struktur* by L. Schäfer). Berkeley is also suspicious of mixing physics and metaphysics and complains "that a certain strange confusion has been introduced into the theory of motion by metaphysical abstractions." Ayers (Ed.), p. 214 (*De motu*, § 16).

[137] E.g. their rejection of an absolute difference between primary and secondary ideas: cf. in *Aim and Structure*, Part II, (Ch. 2, Primary Qualities).

respectively, which are terribly difficult to combine. To the same degree as these difficulties are understood, the position of scientific realism gradually turns into one of scepticism.

Berkeley, who feared scepticism as the preliminary stage for atheism and at the same time wanted to eradicate it from philosophy, had to try to avoid using any kind of representationism in his theories of perception and epistemology: this also applies to the hypotheses that he hinted at himself, namely to those which try to complete our ideas with "archetypes in the divine spirit". Obviously, here the question is raised again whether on the one hand our ("ectypal") ideas are adequately represented, and whether on the other hand they correspond at all with something objective ("archetypes").[138] Berkeley's "participation theory" (remember the cake and its slices in our Chapter I) has to be an uncompromising form of the "direct" theory of perception, if it is not to become entangled in difficulties similar to those associated with the conception it is intended to replace. Thus, taking the strictness of his own philosophy into consideration, we cannot accept Berkeley's liberal information to Samuel Johnson (1696-1772, the "father of American philosophy" and first President of the university later to be named *Columbia University*): "I have no objection against calling the ideas in the mind of God archetypes of ours".[139] The same applies to one of his most original thoughts that only makes sense when it is based on a so-called direct theory of perception. We think that this Berkeleyan idea represents the culmination of his system as it describes the precise point in his philosophy where Berkeley's philosophical metaphysics come into contact with his **personal "mystical belief"**: this is in the thought or **idea of a visible God**.

We encounter this concept at the beginning (*New Theory*) and at the end (*Alciphron*) of his philosophical (in the narrower sense) works. It also forms - this can only be asserted here as it would require a comprehensive analysis of this book to substantiate the claim - the hidden focal point of his mystical late work, *Siris*.[140] Probably this idea also marks the point of contact between the argumentative rational belief and the intuitive view of God in Berkeley's personal religiousness.[141]

---

[138] Cf. in this context Ayers (Ed.) p. 104 (*Principles*, § 88).
[139] Ayers (Ed.), p. 353, 2nd. Letter Berkeley to Johnson, Rhode Island, March 24, 1730.
[140] This forms Vol.5 of *Works in 9 Volumes*. *Siris* and *Alciphron* are not included in Michael Ayers' selection of Berkeley's works.
[141] Friedrich Raab's comment "Berkeley was a relatively irreligious person" is in our opinion contradictory to Berkeley's life **and** writings. Cf. George Berkeley, *Alciphron*, German transl. by Luise Raab and Dr. Friedrich Raab, Leipzig 1915, p. XXVIII ("Introduction of the editor F. Raab").

Even if the author and director of a play stays and works unassumingly back-stage, it is his spirit that lights up the actions and events on-stage. In the same way the existence of God (the creator of nature) and his actions remain hidden from "insensitive eyes":[142] But - of course - not from Berkeley's:

> Look! are not the fields covered with a delightful verdure? Is there not something in the woods and groves, in the rivers and clear springs, that soothes, that delights, that transports the soul? At the prospect of the wide and deep ocean, or some huge mountain whose top is lost in the clouds, or of an old gloomy forest, are not our minds filled with a pleasing horror? Even in rocks and deserts, is there not an agreeable wildness? How sincere a pleasure is it to behold the natural beauties of the earth! [...] Raise now your thoughts from this ball of earth, to all those glorious luminaries that adorn the high arch of heaven [...] How vivid and radiant is the lustre of the fixed stars! How magnificent and rich that negligent profusion, with which they appear to be scattered throughout the whole azure vault![143]

"Insensitive people" do not see things even when their eyes are open (cf. Marc 8,18). However, those who open up themselves for the natural objects we can see, recognize, as if they were looking through a veil, the beauty, richness and magnificence of a divine spirit not completely hidden behind the objects of nature which have been rendered commonplace and "trivial" by our desires for life and survival. Principally, as is clearly shown in the *Principles*, the visual sense does not differ from the other senses. The other senses also reveal some divinity. But these other senses are as it were shrouded by thicker veils and appeal much more directly and urgently to action and life (survival). Only the eye looks up to the stars and is thereby freed at least a little bit from the narrow limitations of our spheres of action and interest.

In the *Theory ... Vindicated and Explained* the idea of a visible God is expressed in a factual and linguistically superior form, although the content is somewhat distorted[144] (as has been already mentioned), by the common ("vulgar") prejudice, according to which the objects of the tactile sense are the things themselves. In *Alciphron*, to which the *New Theory* was added as an appendix, this prejudice remains unchallenged, but in the background, by means of remarks such as: "It puts me in mind of a passage in the Psalmist, where he

---

[142] Cf. Ayers (Ed.), p. 126 (*Principles*, § 154 f.).
[143] Cf. Ayers (Ed.), p. 166 (Second Dialogue, near the beginning).
[144] Cf. e.g. Ayers (Ed.), p. 51 f. (*New Theory*, § 147) and p. 242 (*Theory...Vindicated*, § 43).

represents God to be covered with light as with a garment", this deeper, mystical thread is to be found.[145]. And every attentive reader can detect the obviously intended references to the full or real sense of the idea of a visible God. The sense in the foreground is that the disparity of the various ideas of the different senses poses a problem which cannot be solved purely scientifically. It must be God who relates the visual and tactile ideas through "art". Yet it is not difficult to infer the principal background meaning. The well-regulated co-presence of the different rows of ideas of sense as well as the circumstance that we are at all to perceive ideas of sense, independent of and separate ("ab-solute") from our subjectivity, need to be explained. A material and consciousness-transcending substance is out of the question as *explanans* (as common cause of all these rows). Looking into nature, we see unfathomable beauty together with order, diversity and design. Sometimes we believe that at this sight we "touch" the divine beam of light:[146] are we being too bold when we say that we **see** the explanation that we seek?

---

[145] *Alciphron*, Fourth Dialogue, § 15 (in Luce and Jessop, Eds. Vol. III, p. 162). We also read in this dialogue: "Alciphron: [...] I propound it fairly to your own conscience, whether you really think that God Himself speaks every day and in every place to the eyes of all men. - Euphranor: That ist really and in truth my opinion [...] you have as much reason to think a Universal Agent or God speaks to your eyes, as you can have for thinking any particular person speaks to your eyes." Ibid., p. 157, § 12.

[146] Cf. Ayers (Ed.), p. 126 (*Principles*, § 154): "[...] the divine traces of wisdom and goodness [...] shine throughout the oeconomy of nature."

V. The Theory of Time and Mind (*Philosophical Commentaries*)

V.0. Preliminary remarks

In paragraph 148 of the *Principles* Berkeley starts out with the following impressive sentences:

> It seems to be a general pretence of the unthinking herd, that they cannot see God. Could we but see him, say they, as we see a man, we should believe that he is, and believing obey his commands. But alas we need only open our eyes to see the sovereign Lord of all things with a more full and clear view, than we do any one of our fellow-creatures. [147]

In this final chapter the attempt will be made to present and illuminate Berkeley's thesis concerning our ability to experience things that cannot "justifiably" be experienced at all. In doing this we will find an interesting parallel of his philosophy of religion with his philosophy of the human mind (regarding the experience of the "pure-self"). The most numerous and comprehensive remarks on the subject of "mind and consciousness" are contained in the *Philosophical Commentaries*. They date back to the time Berkeley spent as a student in Dublin and in turning to them we return to the outset of his philosophical work. Thus, the wheel has come to a full circle in our commentary on Berkeley's philosophical writings, as we will not take the late *Siris* into consideration.

Chronologically the *Philosophical Commentaries* represent the beginning, systematically they stand in the centre and "didactically" they form the end of the structure of his ideas. The human mind he discusses there is in a way the most familiar of all "objects" to us. It is the one closest to us (it is us?) and yet it is the very object that is most difficult to grasp and to view clearly. It is this mind that discerns everything - therefore it is itself the most difficult object to discern. We are going to approach it by investigating the phenomena of time. Thus, it is the concept of time, and not that of space, which is the real link or bond between nature and the mind. The philosophy of time is situated where the philosophies of nature and those of the mind converge. As Berkeley himself has not developed this philosophical theory as fully as other ones, we are going to allow ourselves more freedom when describing and interpreting this subject.

---

[147] Ayers (Ed.), p. 124.

V.1. The theory of time in the *Philosophical Commentaries*

In his second letter to Johnson, dated March 24, 1730, Berkeley writes:

> A succession of ideas I take to *constitute* Time, and not to be only the sensible measure thereof, as Mr. Locke and others think. But in these matters every man is to think for himself, and speak as he finds. One of my earliest inquiries was about Time, which led me into several paradoxes that I did not think fit or necessary to publish; particularly the notion that the Resurrection follows the next moment to death. [148]

The quotation tells us a great deal about many aspects of Berkeley's theory of time, in which he regards time as being composed of a sequence of ideas in our consciousness. This implies that time is a variable concept depending on the speed of the change of sequences. However, in this case everyone has "to speak and think for himself". Thus it follows that time according to Berkeley could also be defined differently; an early study of time (possibly primarily in the first pages of the *Philosophical Commentaries*) had produced several "paradoxes", for example, the paradox of the missing interval in between death and resurrection; but this only arises as a consequence of the Berkeleyan consciousness-related concept of time. If we take time to be composed of ideas of consciousness and also take it for granted that no such ideas exist between the idea of being thrown into the "darkness of death" and that of being raised into the "light of a new life", then "time" in Berkeley's sense as described above, could **obviously** not occur between these two ideas.

However, what were the reasons for Berkeley's taking up this eccentric novel version of the concept of time? According to the long philosophical tradition based on Aristotelian philosophy, "time" used to be defined as a "number for measuring movement" (as a measurement of the movements of natural objects in space). In keeping with Newton's theory of relative and absolute time, Locke distinguished between "time" and "duration", defining the latter as "constant, equal, uniform" (Essay II, xiv, 21). Thus, "duration" is the real, or "absolute" time which cannot be "put out of time (rythm)", so-to-speak, by the sequence of ideas and their varying "speed". In contrast, "time" is ideal, itself being constituted of individual (subjectiv) ideas of consciousness. This is also the terminological starting point for the discussion of time at the beginning of the *Commentaries*. Here we read for example:

---

[148] Ayers (Ed.), p. 354.

4. Time train of ideas succeeding each other.
7. Why time in pain, longer than time in pleasure?
8. Duration infinitely divisible, time not so. [149]

Therefore time cannot be divided infinitely because it consists of sequences of ideas and these ideas cannot be shortened at random. Take for example two flashes of light rapidly following each other. After a certain period of time we do no longer perceive them as separate entities, but as one single flash of light. Experience tells us that the point where the two lights coincide may vary slightly from person to person. However, there is a much greater difference between the perceptions of man and that of different animals. In this case it follows naturally that as in paragraph (or "commentary") 48 "the age of a fly for ought that we know may be as long as y^t of a man." [150] **Age** is to be understood as a span of (subjective) time and not as a span of (objective) duration, although Berkeley there does not specifically say so. Starting with this omission, his conception of time begins to deviate from that of Locke and that of the layman and starts to show the "eccentric traits" mentioned above. Thus, in his later entries of the *Commentaries* Berkeley pretends in many respects that objective duration does not really exist at all and that this concept had never even been discussed by him ... We are given the impression that to the same degree that his immaterialistic denial of (material) objects in themselves appears to be theoretically manifest, he also is no longer interested in a concept of time that is transcendental of (subjective) ideas. Three typical examples of this are:

> [Firstly] 390. Marsilius ficinus his appearing the moment he died solv'd by my idea of time. [151]

Michele Mercatius reported that his friend, the Humanist scholar Ficinius (Ficino), appeared to him at the moment of his death in 1490. He appeared at a place different from that of his death to ensure his friend that there is life after life. The riddle of how one person can be in two places at the same time would be solved, if time were only composed of a succession of ideas in the conscious mind(s) of individual subjects. Thus time for Mercatius would be different from to that of the people who were present at Ficinus' deathbed.

> [Secondly] 590. No broken Intervals of Death or Annihilation. Those Intervals are nothing. Each Person's time being measured to him by his own Ideas. [152]

---

[149] Ayers (Ed.), p. 253. (The commentary-numbers at the beginning of each proposition should make work with other editions than Ayers' easier.)
[150] Ayers (Ed.), p. 256.
[151] Ayers (Ed.), p. 286.

Berkeley was probably referring to the "paradoxical" thought that underlay this entry in the already quoted letter that he wrote to Johnson about 23 years later. Only the phrase "to him" might possibly be the cause for some doubts as to our theory of Berkeley's disregard of time as objective duration. However, if we take the following series of entries into consideration, all doubts which may arise can be quietened for the time being.

[Thirdly] 650. Locke seems to be mistaken w^n he says thought is not essential to the mind.

651. Certainly the mind always & constantly thinks & we know this too. In Sleep & trances the mind exists not there is no time no succession of Ideas.

652. To say the mind exists' without thinking is a Contradiction, nonsense, nothing. [153]

Here, in the face of Locke's criticism, Berkeley does not only adopt once more the old Cartesian idea of a perpetually active mind, but also radicalizes it by claiming that it is an **analytic truth**. The prerequisite for this is none other than the determined acclamation of the "eccentric"-subjective time conception. Johnson had put before Berkeley the question of whether it was possible to speak of a person "John" who is fast asleep in the following way: "He isn't thinking but he continues to exist." Ordering the concept "thoughts" to his generic term "ideas", Berkeley answers (see abow and below) by saying that "time" is not only measured by the succession of John's ideas but that it is also **constituted** by it. In keeping with this concept it follows that time cannot exist for John without this (his) succession of ideas. Thus "John's mind is always thinking" is true because "always" as a word has no meaning for John if it is considered irrespective of (or abstracted from) his ideas. All this leads to the conclusion that different people or different conscious beings experience different times and that even different "eternities" exist! This is the way the first entry of the *Commentaries*, the very first historically recorded remark of Berkeley's at all, should be understood: "1. One eternity greater than another of ye same kind." [154] But can this practically solipsistic view of time and eternity really be Berkeley's final word?

That there is a general tendency towards solipsism in Berkeley's thought is clear [...] When Berkeley writes about time, particularly in the

---

[152] Ayers (Ed.), p. 308.
[153] Ayers (Ed.), p. 314.
[154] Ayers (Ed.), p. 253.

Commentaries, we find the subjectivist and solipsistic tendency in his thinking at its strongest.[155]

Although each of us only experiences his (her) own time, the bishop can assume that other people are in turn experiencing their own times. "Time in itself" is for Berkeley an unjustified abstraction as it seems to disregard the way in which time originally occurs in the consciousness. There are several indications that he shared Kant's opinion that it would be impossible to abstract time from an external or internal experience - in other words - time is somehow a kind of original ("innate") condition of the (finite) consciousness. This thought can be traced in the entry (again quite Cartesian) immediately preceding the sequence of passages 650-652 already quoted, which are so crucial for our understanding of his time concept.: "649. There are innate Ideas i.e. Ideas created with us."[156]

Taking into consideration the whole context of the time discussion, the following interpretation seems plausible: one of these "Ideas created with us" is time.[157]

If Berkeley really regarded time as an "idea" (or a species of ideas, a sensation), we should hardly be surprised that he was only prepared to accept it as an integral part of a conscious mind. Paragraph 13 of the *Commentaries* provides us with decisive proof of this assumption: "13. Time a sensation, therefore onely in ye mind".[158] Here we can find a hint in the direction of a negative answer to the still-open question of whether the "almost solipsistic concept of time and eternity" really was Berkeley's last word. We have already known for some time that Berkeley did not want **ideas** to be interpreted subjectively - on the contrary, for him they exist in the mind of God. Now could not the same apply to the "sensations" (ideas) of time as well? This question has to be discussed separately and at greater length.

V.2. Time and Divinity

In the passage quoted above from his letter to Johnson, Berkeley argues that his early studies of the time concept had led to paradoxical consequences. Could it possibly be that one of these consequences has to do with the following dilemma?

---

[155] I. C. Tipton, *Berkeley, The Philosophy of Immaterialism*, London 1974, p. 278.
[156] Ayers (Ed.), p. 313 (however, the preceding § 647, in Ayers' edition on the same page, reads rather different. Berkeley often corrects his own argument with a short counter-argument.
[157] Later Berkeley refers to the "ideas created with us" as "notions".
[158] Ayers (Ed.), p. 253.

There is no more point in stopping at a purely subjectivist concept of time, according to which every being endowed with a mind is living "in" his own individual time, than in adopting a solipsist concept where time, or respectively the perception of time, exist purely in one individual only. Working on both principles, the most everyday occurrence, such as keeping an appointment at a predetermined (place and) time, appears to be a wonder or sheer miracle (Berkeley takes such an event for granted for example in § 97 of the *Principles*: "Bid your servant meet you at such a *time* [...]").[159] George Pitcher refers to such eccentric ideas of time as "a total disaster" and continues:

> I think the view is in fact incomprehensible. It states that there is no single time series, but a host of separate times; one for each mind. There is your time, my time, Bunny's time, and so on. But can we understand the expressions "your time", "my time", Bunny's time", when they are specifically *not* meant to be referring to such things as Pacific Coast Time or London Time, but rather to just *time* (in general)? I do not think we can. When you and I are living in the same time zone, what could be meant by speaking of "your Tuesday", "my Tuesday" and so on? Your Tuesday *is* my Tuesday - and indeed, quite generally, as Rudy Vallee used wisely to point out, your time is my time. It is Bunny's time, too. The point is this: the conception of a real world is the conception of one in which (real) events are ordered temporally in a commonway, the same for all people.[160]

Pitcher's humorous remarks might be countered by pointing out that for Berkeley the constant processes of motion in nature are sufficient for explaining how we manage to keep appointments. The bishop and his servant do have their own individual "times", but in case they have arranged to meet in front of the mayor's house in Cloyne at noon for example, they can both orientate themselves by checking the position of the sun or that of the hands of a church-clock. However inviting this idea may be, unfortunately it does not at all take us very far. If there are motional processes in the world that can be perceived and - in a broader sense - measured by both men, then both, the subjective times **and** the objective points of time exist. The latter are indeed traditionally interpreted as being the very measurements of such motions - and they have been explicitly denied by Berkeley. And would not Berkeley himself surely point out that not only this (objective) time does exist in truth as a sensation or group of sensual ideas only in the servant's and bishops minds, but also that the sun or the church-clock are in a similar way primarily groups of sensations

---

[159] Ayers (Ed.), p. 107.
[160] George Pitcher, *Berkeley*. op. cit., p. 209..

existing in the individual mind of each particular person? So the fact seems to remain that we cannot stop at the purely subjective concept of time as the individual sensation of sequences of ideas.

On the other hand Berkeley is utterly convinced that it is impossible to approach (or even embrace) the "ordinary" concept of objective or even absolute time: "Time [...] being nothing, abstracted from the succession of ideas in our minds".[161] More precisely, time is for him supposedly a kind of "innate basic part" of our consciousness itself and it is therefore not possible to think of it objectively as if we were detached from it. According to Berkeley, time is essentially **awareness of time**, and time does not exist at all if it is not the kind of time which seems to pass slowly in times of sorrow and fast in times of joy.[162] As far as the ideas of sense are concerned, the desired solution to this problem is found by referring to the awareness and mind of God. It seems to us that Berkeley thinks that the ideas of sense, of which the church-clock and the sun consist, are also and above all to be found in the mind of God. The ideas of sense, being the "true atoms of nature", continue to exist in His mind when my mind or any other mind is not watching, listening etc. Cannot Berkeley say that the same applies to time (times) and especially to duration as well? Admittedly this seems rather questionable at first and the divine spirit is traditionally not associated with temporality and transitiveness at all. Berkeley's **dilemma** is thus that he can neither stop with this subjectivist or even solipsist concept of time, nor go beyond it as both the directions towards "natural" objectivism and, in the case of time at least, theism seem to be blocked.

The assumption that the path to theism is blocked obviously needs to be discussed in greater depth. In the *Dialogues* Philonous explains that God "knows and comprehends" the things we experience as ideas of sense:

> Now it is plain they [the objects of our experience, S. B.] have an exterior to my mind, since I find them by experience to be independent of it. There is therefore some other mind wherein they exist, during the intervals between the times of my perceiving them: as likewise they did before my birth and would do after my supposed annihilation. And as the same is true, with regard to all other finite created spirits; it necessarily follows, there is an *omnipresent eternal mind*, which knows and comprehends all things, and exhibits them to our view in such a manner, and according to such rules as he himself hath ordained, and are by us termed the *Laws of nature*.[163]

---

[161] Ayers (Ed.), p. 107 (*Principles*, § 98).
[162] Cf. the very beginning of the *Commentaries*. In: Ayers (Ed.), p. 253.
[163] Ayers (Ed.), p. 183 (Third Dialogue).

A little later in the text Hylas reconsiders the manner in which things exist in God. Assuming that it would be absurd to say that God is able to suffer pain, he thinks he can counter Berkeley-Philonous in using the argument that all the ideas in our minds are also in God's mind; however, we sometimes have very unpleasant ideas called "pains", thus ... Philonous responds in the following way:

> That God knows or understands all things, and that He knows among other things what pain is, even every sort of painful sensation, and what it is for His creatures to suffer pain, I make no question. But that God, though He knows and sometimes causes painful sensations in us, can Himself suffer pain, I positively deny. [164]

To summarize briefly: Berkeley comes to the conclusion, as Augustine already in the eleventh book of his *Confessiones* did, that time "passes" in each man's own mind and that the mind (and here especially memory) is a prerequisite for its measurement. [165] The question is only whether, in addition to this subjective kind of time, an objective duration of time has to be assumed. However, as Berkeley refuses to believe that objective duration of time could be absolute or indeed existed at all "in itself", the question is put whether it is possible for the idea of duration to be in the mind of God. At this point the fear emerges that the two concepts of "duration" and "mind of God" may be incommensurable - as it is not possible for us to think of any kind of temporality (not even an "objective" kind) in connection with this mind. Looking into the *Dialogues*, we are shown how Berkeley deals with the difficulties that arise from the idea that such very human and very worldly sensations as pain are to be found in the mind of God. The solution to the problem lies in the distinction between "feeling pain (or time)" and "knowing pain (or time)". Thus Berkeley has a way out of the apparent dilemma mentioned above as he is able to say that because **God knows objective duration, it really does exist**. Does not that mean, however, that we are fixing God in time? No, it does not, because what God knows must not be regarded as being an actual part of God himself. The content of the mind and the mind (spirit) itself are two distinguishable entities. Berkeley's writings give us no indication as to **how** objective duration of time exists in God's mind. Obviously, he thinks (most plausibly) that we are unable to imagine it. Despite this the fact remains that an objective duration is possibly conceivable within the framework of the

---

[164] Ayers (Ed.), p. 190 (Third Dialogue).
[165] "In te, anime meus, tempora metior. Noli mihi obstrepere: quod est; noli mihi obstrepere turbis affecionum tuarum. In te, inquam, tempora metior. Affecionem, quam res praetereuntes in te faciunt et, cum illae praeterierint, manet, ipsam metior praesentem, non ea quae praeterierunt ut fieret; ipsam metior, cum tempora metior. Ergo aut ipsa sunt tempora, aut non tempora metior." *Confessiones*, 11th Book, 27, 36 (various editions).

immaterialistic philosophy - even if this goes against Berkeley's own original (juvenile) claims.

Sometimes the personal intentions of the author of a systematically developed construction of ideas are dominated by the (hidden or partly-hidden) consequences inherent in the chosen approach. This applies to the philosopher under discussion here. Originally Berkeley was of the opinion that pure empiricism is enough - also for a theistic thinker. Later he had to draw a clear line between thinking in concepts (notions) and understanding through perception processes and ideas. Thus, the objectivistic elements of Berkeley's philosophy, i.e. the "theistic" elements, make it impossible for him to insist on pure empiricism. In this context the discrimination of "notions" from "ideas" results in a division of human cognitive capacity. Berkeley distinguishes between an innate intellectual basic equipment (including the notion of time) and the contents of the mind gained through sensual experience. (This of course foreshadows Kants "Transcendental Aesthetics".)

V.3. Berkeley's conception of the mind and the "Lockean objection"

The writings of Bishop Berkeley, the often so-called "spiritualist", reveal very little about spirit or mind. This may merely be due to chance as the manuscript of the second part of the *Principles* which concerned mainly the mind, was lost in Italy in 1718.[166] But it may also have more systematic reasons. Considering the contents of his philosophy, the latter explanation seems even more reasonable. The mind or the subject of knowledge perceives everything and can thus not be the object of perception itself. Schopenhauer, who had already referred to George Berkeley's "immortal contribution to philosophy" in the very first paragraph of his work *Die Welt als Wille und Vorstellung*, adds in the following paragraph:

> Dasjenige, was Alles erkennt und von Keinem erkannt wird ist das Subjekt. Es ist sonach der Träger der Welt, die durchgängige, stets vorausgesetzte Bedingung alles Erscheinenden, alles Objekts: denn nur für das Subjekt ist, was nur immer da ist. Als dieses Subjekt findet Jeder sich selbst, jedoch nur sofern er Objekt der Erkenntnis ist, Objekt ist aber schon sein Leib, welchen selbst wir daher, von diesem Standpunkt aus, Vorstellung nennen. Denn der Leib ist Objekt unter Objekten und den Gesetzen der Objekte unterworfen, obwohl er unmittelbares Objekt ist. Er liegt, wie alle Objekte der Anschauung, in den Formen allen Erkennens, in Zeit und Raum, durch welche die Vielheit ist. Das Subjekt aber, das

---

[166] Cf. Ayers (Ed.), p. 347, Berkeley's first letter to Johnson (near the end).

Erkennende, nie Erkannte, liegt auch nicht in diesen Formen, von denen selbst es vielmehr immer schon vorausgesetzt wird: ihm kommt also weder Vielheit, noch deren Gegensatz, Einheit, zu. Wir erkennen es nimmer, sondern es eben ist es, das erkennt, wo nur erkannt wird. [167]

The subject is known as being "da-seiend" and not "wie-seiend". This is certainly the way in which Berkeley saw the matter. Schopenhauer adhered to these remarks by commenting that even such basic concepts as "unity" and "multiplicity" cannot be applied in any attempt of explaining the subject. This is an interesting comment we should bear it in mind during the following discussion of Berkeley's concept of the subjectivity.

Although we have just been using the words **"mind"**and **"subject** at random, it is advisable to make a distinction. This has already been done in this interpretation, not as regards the terminology used, but the contents and general meaning: the differentiation between the subject or self as the enduring (time-constituting) "point" where everything which is experienced is bound together on the one hand, and the area of consciousness or the content of the individual "point" or subject on the other hand. It is necessary for us to make such distinctions in terminology if we are to avoid getting confused whilst studying Berkeley's writing. We can read on the one hand for example:

> 701. The substance of Body we know, the substance of Spirit we do not know it not being knowable, it being purus actus. [168]

- and -

> Hence there can be no idea formed of a soul or spirit: for all ideas whatever, being passive and inert, [...] they cannot represent unto us, by way of image or likenesse, that which acts. [169]

The subject of the mind is being referred to here and we are told it is unrecognizable because of its very nature as an act (actus purus). On the other hand we can read:

> It is evident to anyone who takes a survey of the objects of human knowledge, that they are either ideas actually imprinted on the senses, or else such as are perceived by attending to the passions and operations of the mind, or lastly ideas formed by help of memory and imagination, [...] [170]

---

[167] Arthur Schopenhauer, *Die Welt als Wille und Vorstellung* I, § 2 (various editions).
[168] Ayers (Ed.), p. 319.
[169] Ayers (Ed.), p. 85 (*Principles*, § 27).
[170] Ayers (Ed.), p. 77 (*Principles*, § 1).

revealed to himself in the freedom of his will (and to others "in" his face and eyes). The "shining" beauty of nature, the freedom of will and the "shining" of eyes are facts of our consciousness. Thus they are at the same time the means by which we can "experience" spiritual being. Therefore we have to say that we do not only (or so much) rationally discover the transcendent, but rather that "it" is shown to us.

Conclusion

"We see God": George Berkeley's apodictic and in itself enigmatic thesis from the *Principles of Human Knowledge*, section 148, contains the core for a new interpretation of his five main philosophical works, *Principles* (chap. 1), *Three Dialogues Between Hylas und Philonous* (chap. 2), *The New Theory of Vision* (chap. 3), *On Motion* (chap. 4), and *Philosophical Commentaries* (chap.5). Taking serious the religious aspect of his philosophical thinking this interpretation can also claim to agree for the first time with the author's, the Irish Arch Bishop's, original intentions.

This intentions are the more remarkable for the fact that the famous philosopher was at the same time an influential historical figure in political and public life. Thus, any interpretation of his literary-philosophical aims at the same time means trying to clear up this part in Anglo-Saxon history he participated in. Conversely, taking into consideration his political plans (e.g. the project to build a College for missionaries in Bermuda, which was fiercly dabated in Parliament, eventually consented to, but finally refused financial support) a characteristic light is thrown on his philosophical work, which can really be understood as "apologetic" in a broader sense. Berkeley's thesis of "God's visibility" in nature moreover reveals him a "mystic of nature". This opinion represents a significant addition to the sensualistic view of Berkeley which is widely held; it does not contradict the characterization of the philosopher as a "philosopher of experience" fundamentally though. Nevertheless, there are also non-empirical elements of an intuitionist kind in particular in Berkeley's epistemology, philosophy of language, and metaphysics. In the first place, however, the almost general misconception of Berkeley's "immaterialism" as a form of "subjective idealism", which at least can be traced back to Reid and Kant, must be firmly rejected. Usually, Berkeley not only acknowledges an autonomous realm of nature - which to him is above all that of corporeal things in space and time - he even believes to be able to expierience in it (as in his fellow-subjects) intuitiv, through visual perception, a mind that is different from his own (and which eventually is not "projected" into nature)! In his essay "L'intuition philosophique" on Berkeley's immaterialism, Henri Bergson already remarked that corporeal nature is not simply denied but rather taken as a (kind of) transparent skin, which is extended between God's infinite and man's finite spirit. We believe that, together with Bergson, we have discoverd in this picture the original intuition of the great thinker of the late baroque period.

Immaterialism, when seen in this perspective, appears to be a largely unified whole, that is, its single components, like the argument for the existence of God (chap. 1), the theory of objects (chap. 2), the theory of perception (chap. 3), the theory of science (chap. 4), and the theory of mind (chap. 5) maintain and support each other in a way which is almost "organic". - By that, the question of the truth of this philosophy becomes relevant again: it has been practically meaningless as long as immaterialism was misunderstood as subjectiv idealism. This question of truth, regardless of its formal simplicity, appears to be extremely difficult to answer: it is almost identical with posing all the fundamental philosophical problems! Nevertheless, our previous discussion ventured a few steps into this area. It was found that Berkeley's critique of naive realism (as it is called) is indeed worthwhile being taken seriously. We think that the same is still true for his "new" theory of vision, which, of course, would need further amplification. It is true that, systematically, Berkeley's antirealist theory of science is very closely related to his intuitionist "natural" mysticism (i.e. his experience of God's working in nature), in itself, however, it is doubtlessly questionable, as progress in science always means an increase in knowledge, too. The argument for the existence of God is unprecedented in the history of philosophy and theology, and "original" in the word's full sense, although it fails to convince as regards content; but the precise mistake in its logic, if there really slipped in one, has probably still to be found out and determined more accurately. While looking back at the first chapter of our study may be dissappointing presently as regards "systematic" content, looking back at the final one, in contrast, may be more pleasant: Berkeley's theses concerning topics of time, consciousness, time-consciousness, self-consciousness, substantial person, freedom and divinity, which are reconstructed there, are still worth - like much more that flew from the pen of this probably greatest Irish thinker - being discussed, and being pondered over.

Zusammenfassung in deutscher Sprache

"Wir sehen Gott": George Berkeleys apodiktische und, für sich betrachtet, änigmatische Aussage aus Abschnitt 148 seiner *Prinzipien der menschlichen Erkenntnis* (1710) enthält den Keim für eine neue Deutung seiner fünf philosophischen Hauptwerke - *Prinzipien* (Kap. 1), *Drei Dialoge zwischen Hylas und Philonous* (Kap. 2), *Die neue Theorie des Sehens* (Kap. 3), *Über Bewegung* (Kap. 4) und *Philosophisches Tagebuch* (Kap. 5). Diese Interpretation kann, indem sie den religiösen Aspekt seines Philosophierens erstmalig wirklich ernst nimmt, überdies für sich geltend machen, daß sie auch erstmals mit den ureigenen Intentionen ihres Verfassers, des irischen Erzbischofs, übereinstimmt.

Diese Intentionen verdienen umso mehr Beachtung, als es sich bei dem berühmten Philosophen zugleich um eine einflußreiche historische Gestalt des politischen und öffentlichen Lebens handelte. Jede Deutung seiner philosophisch-literarischen Absichten und Ziele stellt damit zugleich den Versuch einer Erhellung eines, durch ihn mitbestimmten, Stückes angelsächsischer Geschichte dar. Umgekehrt wirft auch die Beachtung seiner politischen Pläne (z.B. das mehrfach heftig vor dem Parlament diskutierte, schließlich genehmigte, dann doch nicht finanziell unterstützte Projekt der Errichtung einer Missionarsschule auf den Bermuda-Inseln) ein bezeichnendes Licht auf seine philosophische Arbeit, welche - in einem weiteren Sinne - durchaus als "apologetisch" bezeichnet werden kann. Seine These von der "Sichtbarkeit Gottes" in der Natur weist Berkeley aber auch - wiederum in einem weiteren Sinne - als (Natur-)Mystiker aus. Diese Auffassung stellt eine gewichtige Ergänzung für ein verbreitetes sensualistisches "Berkeley-Bild" dar, ohne soweit grundsätzlich der Charakterisierung dieses Denkers als einem "Erfahrungs-Philosophen" zu widersprechen. Allerdings gibt es auch nicht-empirische Elemente, insb. intuitionistischer Art, in Berkeleys Erkenntnislehre, Sprachphilosophie und Metaphysik. Vor allem muß jedoch einem beinahe generellen Mißverständnis des Berkeleyschen "Immaterialismus" als einer Form von "subjektivem Idealismus", wie es zumindest bis auf Reid und Kant zurückgeführt werden kann, entschieden entgegengetreten werden. Berkeley erkennt gewöhnlich ein eigenständiges Reich der Natur - d.h. für ihn v.a. der Körperdinge in Raum und Zeit - nicht nur an: Er glaubt darin sogar, wie in seinen Mitmenschen, einen anderen als den eigenen (evtl. in die Natur "hineinprojizierten") Geist, visuell wahr-nehmend, intuitiv erfahren zu können! Wie schon Bergson in seinem Essay "L'intuition philosophique" über den Berkeleyschen Immaterialismus schrieb, wird die körperliche Natur darin nicht einfachhin geleugnet, sondern eher wie ein "durchsichtiges Häutchen" aufgefaßt, das zwischen den unendlichen Geist Gottes und den endlichen Geist des Menschen ausgespannt ist. Zusammen mit Bergson glauben auch wir in diesem Bild sozusagen die "Urintuition" des großen spätbarocken Denkers gefunden zu haben.

Unter dieser Perspektive betrachtet, stellt sich der "Immaterialismus" als ein in sich weitgehend geschlossenes Ganze dar; d.h. die einzelnen Bestandteile, wie Gottesbeweis (Kap. 1), Körperlehre (Kap. 2), Wahrnehmungslehre (Kap. 3), Wissenschaftstheorie (Kap. 4) und Theorie des Geistes (Kap. 5) stützen und erhalten einander auf geradezu "organische" Weise. - Damit wird offensichtlich auch die Frage nach der Wahrheit dieser Philosophie aktuell: Eine Frage, welche solange praktisch bedeutungslos gewesen ist, wie der Immaterialismus als subjektiver Idealismus mißverstanden wurde. Diese Wahrheitsfrage ist, bei aller formalen Schlichtheit, offenbar äußerst schwierig zu beantworten (sie wäre beinahe mit einer Beantwortung der philosophischen Grundfragen identisch!), dennoch sind im Vorhergehenden auch einige Schritte in diese Richtung gewagt worden. Dabei ergab sich, daß es Berkeleys Kritik am sog. naiven Realismus in der Erkenntnistheorie durchaus verdiente, ernst genommen zu werden. Dasselbe gilt u.E. auch noch immer von seiner - freilich ergänzungsbedürftigen - "neuen" Theorie der visuellen Wahrnehmung. Berkeleys anti-realistische Wissenschaftstheorie steht zwar im engsten, systematischen Zusammenhang mit seiner intuitionistischen "Naturmystik" (seiner Erfahrung von Gottes Wirken in der Natur), ist aber zweifellos für sich genommen sehr fragwürdig, bedeutet der Fortschritt der Naturwissenschaften doch immer auch einen sukzessiven Erkenntnisgewinn. Der in der Philosophie- und Theologiegeschichte beispiellose Gottesbeweis ist im besten Wortsinne "originell", vermag aber inhaltlich ebenfalls nicht ganz zu überzeugen, wobei eventuell noch genauer festzustellen wäre, wo sich wirklich ein Denkfehler eingeschlichen hat. Im Gegensatz zu diesem, in jetziger inhaltlicher Sichtweise, vielleicht enttäuschenden Rückblick auf das erste Kapitel unserer Studie, dürfte der Rückblick auf das letzte diesbezüglich erfreulicher ausfallen: Berkeleys darin rekonstruierte Thesen zu den Themen Zeit, Bewußtsein, Zeitbewußtsein, Selbstbewußtsein, substanzielle Person, Freiheit und Göttlichkeit sind - wie vieles andere aus der Feder des wahrscheinlich größten irischen Denkers - auch heute noch diskussionswürdig und, im besten Wortsinn, bedenkenswert.

Literature

AYERS, Michael R. (Ed.), BERKELEY: Philosophical Works Including the Works on Vision, London 1985[5] (= Primary literature)

The same: "Divine Ideas and Berkeley's Proofs of God's Existence", in: Sosa, E. (Ed.), Essays on the Philosophy of George Berkeley, Boston 1987

BENNETT, Jonathan, Locke-Berkeley-Hume: Central Themes, Oxford 1971

BERMAN, David, "Cognitive Theology and Emotive Mysteries in Berkeley's 'Alciphron', in: *Royal Irish Academy*, 1981

The same: Meaning and Method in Berkeley's Theology, Trinity College Dublin 1972 (Ph.D.-thesis, unpublished)

BERGSON, Henri, Oevres (ed. by H. Gouhier), Paris 1963

BRACKEN, Harry M., Berkeley, London 1974

BRYKMAN, Geneviève, Berkeley et le voile des mots, Paris 1993

CLARK, Stephen R.C., "God - Appointed Berkeley and the General Good", in: John Foster and Howard Robinson (Eds.), Essays on Berkeley: A Tercennial Celebration, Oxford 1985

DUHEM, Pierre, The Aim and Structure of Physical Theory, New York 1962

GUEROULT, Martial, Berkeley: Quatre études sur la perception et sur dieu, Paris 1956

HEESS, Manfred, Blaise Pascal: Wissenschaftliches Denken und Christlicher Glaube, München 1977

HUME, David, The Philosophical Works in 4 Volumes (ed. by Th.G. Hill and Th.H.Grose), London 1986 (Repr. Aalen 1992)

HUSSERL, Edmund, Ideen zu einer reinen Phänomenologie und phänomenologischen Philosophie (ed. by E. Ströker), Hamburg 1992

The same: Erste Philosophie (ed. by E. Ströker), Hamburg 1992

The same: Logische Untersuchungen (ed. by E. Ströker), Hamburg 1992

KING; Edward J., "Language, Berkeley and God", in: Creery, W.E. (Ed.), George Berkeley: Critical Assessments, Vol. 1, London 1991

KLEMMT, Alfred (Ed.), George Berkeley: Eine Abhandlung über die Prinzipien der menschlichen Erkenntnis (German edition of the "Principles"), Hamburg 1979[3]

KLINE, David A., "Berkeley's Divine Language Argument", in: Sosa, E. (Ed.), Essays on the Philosophy of George Berkeley, Dordrecht 1987

KULENKAMPFF, Arend, George Berkeley, Munich 1987

LEIBNIZ, G.W., Specimen dynamicum, Acta Eraditorum 1965 (different new editions)

LOCKE, John, The Works in 10 Volumes, London 1823

LUCE, Aslon A., Berkeley's Immaterialism, New York 1964[2]

The same: Berkeley and Malebranche, Oxford 1967

LUCE, Aston A. and JESSOP Thomas E. (Eds.), George Berkeley, Bishop of Cloyne: The Works in 9 Volumes, London 1964[2] (= Primary literature)

LYON, George, L'idéalism en angleterre au dix-huitième siècle, Paris 1988

MACKIE, John L., The Miracle of Theism, Oxford 1982

The same: Problems from Locke, Oxford 1976

MALEBRANCHE, Nicholas, Oevres (ed. by G. Rodis-Lewis), Paris 1962-1964

McCRACKEN, Charles, "What Does Berkeley's God See in the Quad ?", in: *Archiv für Geschichte der Philosophie*, 1979

METZGER, Wolfgang, Gesetze des Sehens, Frankfurt/Main 1973[3]

OLSCAMP, Paul J., The Moral Philosophy of George Berkeley, The Hague 1970

PITCHER, George, Berkeley, London 1984[2]

POLITZ, Alfred, On the Origin of Space Perception, in: *Philosophy and Phenomenological Research* 40 (1979/80), pp. 258-264

POPPER, Karl R., "A Note on Berkeley as a Precursor of Mach", in: *The British Journal for the Philosophy of Science* 4 (1954), pp. 26-36

RAAB, Friedrich (Ed.), George Berkeley: Alciphron (German edition), Leipzig 1915

ROCK, Irvin, Perception, New York 1984

SCHOPENHAUER, Arthur, Werke in zehn Bänden ("Zurich Edition"), Zürich 1977

von SENDEN, Marius, Raum- und Gestaltauffassung von operierten Blindgeborenen, Leipzig 1932

TIPTON, I.C., Berkeley: The Philosophy of Immaterialism, London 1974

URMSON, James O., Berkeley, Oxford 1983

WARNOCK, G.J., Berkeley, Oxford 1983[3]

WENZ, Peter S., "Berkeley's Christian Neo-Platonism", in: Creery, W.E. (Ed.), George Berkeley: Critical Assessments, Vol. 2, London 1991